5.75 net.

Hector Berlioz

HECTOR BERLIOZ

RATIONAL ROMANTIC

by John Crabbe

KAHN & AVERILL
LONDON

First published in 1980 by Stanmore Press Ltd
under their associated imprint: Kahn & Averill

British Library Cataloguing in Publication Data.

Crabbe, John
  Hector Berlioz.
  1. Berlioz, Hector
  2. Composers - France - Biography
  780'.92'4   ML410.B5

  ISBN 0-900707-53-4

Printed and Bound in Great Britain by
REDWOOD BURN LIMITED
Trowbridge & Esher

Contents

Acknowledgements 7

Preface 9

1 — Casting the Spiritual Mould 15

2 — Disbelieving Rationalist 21

3 — A Religion of Feeling 27

4 — Composer as Social Critic 37

5 — How to Change the World 42

6 — Romantic Disillusion 48

7 — A Celtic Backcloth 58

8 — Sounds of the Spirit 68

9 — Intellectual at Large 77

10 — Influences and Attitudes 84

11 — Slaying the Philistine Devil 93

12 — A Secular Holy Trinity 99

13 — The Creative Imagination 107

Appendix: The Emmet Connection 113

References 129

Bibliography 133

Index 137

Acknowledgements

I wish to thank the following authors and their publishers for permission to reprint excerpts from English translations of Berlioz texts and several other items. David Cairns for numerous passages from his splendid version of the *Memoirs* (Gollancz); also from pieces by him in *Berlioz and the Romantic Imagination* (Arts Council), *Responses* (Martin Secker & Warburg), and *Evenings in the Orchestra* (Penguin, ed: Fortescue). Professor Jacques Barzun has been a prolific source of quotations, with many passages coming from *Berlioz and the Romantic Century* (Gollancz); also several from *Evenings with the Orchestra* (Chicago U.P.) and *New Letters of Berlioz* (Columbia U.P.). Humphrey Searle's *Hector Berlioz — a Selection from his Letters* (Gollancz) has been used, and also Edwin Evans' version of *A Travers Chants* (Reeves). Three other sources of translations printed here are: *Letters of Composers through six centuries* (Chilton Book Co., ed: Piero Weiss); *The Musician's World* (Thames & Hudson, ed: Hans Gal); and *Adam International Review* (University of Rochester, ed: Miron Grindea).

A few further isolated Berlioz comments and some items from classics or other books now out of copyright join all the above in my list of References and/or the Bibliography, while the latter includes all those books I have found useful when seeking background information on Berlioz and his time. Some English versions of passages from the composer's vocal music have been taken from performing scores, or from word sheets issued with recordings. Thanks are also due to Professor Ian Stevenson, Dr. Hugh Macdonald and Winton

Dean for permission to reprint short original passages from, respectively, *Twenty Cases Suggestive of Reincarnation* (American Soc. P.R.), *Berlioz Orchestral Music* (BBC), and *Shakespeare in Music* (Macmillan, ed: Hartnoll).

I have received generous assistance from many friends and colleagues in the search for elusive pieces of Berlioziana, and from others who have assisted in practical ways. Daphne Baker has been paramount in the latter, coping at her ever-ready typewriter with much dreadful handwriting and constant changes of mind. Basil Ashmore offered helpful comments on an early draft of the text. Hugh Macdonald, Richard Macnutt, Julian Rushton, John Warrack, Katherine Kolb and Ian Kemp have clarified various small points, especially in relation to the sources of Berlioz's vocal texts, and Mr. Kemp also provided a thematic analysis for the musical parody mentioned in the Appendix. Ian Martin has been very helpful on bibliographical matters in English; likewise Cosette Comboroure in French, especially concerning links between France and Ireland. Leon O'Broin has also been helpful on Irish matters. Professor Beat Junker of the Swiss Historical Society confirmed certain travel routes into SE France, and the French Military Attaché in London obtained data on Napoleonic troop movements. Finally, David Cairns has been my mentor on every conceivable aspect of Hector Berlioz and a notably sympathetic and positive critic from beginning to end. My heartfelt thanks to all these good people, none of whom is implicated in any of my opinions, or in the precarious ideas on the Irish connection discussed in the Appendix.

J.C.

Preface

This book is a venture into a new sort of biography, an investigation of the ideas, beliefs and feelings of a creative artist. The composer Hector Berlioz is set here within a nexus of social, political, religious and literary influences to illuminate the mind behind his music. With poets or philosophers the study of a man's work may be tantamount to a survey of his mind, but no other type of great creator seems to have been examined in the manner adopted here, which is to plot the spiritual and intellectual framework in which genius has its being — to provide a tour through the world of verbal ideas as mirrored within the mind of a man famed for his non-verbal art.

The author has always been curious to learn about the feelings and beliefs of any great pioneer of the human spirit, especially concerning the big questions of religion, politics, philosophy and the meaning of existence. But one is easily frustrated when gathering such information, for this generally involves assembling snippets of data from a multitude of sources. However, with the conviction that a knowledge of such things should not only help to throw new light on the roots of a man's art, but perhaps also tell us something about the mechanism of creativity itself, this study has been compiled. Another motivating ingredient is a deep interest in the rôle of ideas and beliefs in history, and in the case of Berlioz a special concern with the way in which art and ideology became intermingled in the Romantic age.

Berlioz can be regarded as the first 'pure' romantic; pure in the sense that he had no personal roots in the classical

Viennese tradition of Haydn and Mozart — preferring the
dramatic lineage of Gluck and Weber — and romantic in his
belief that music can and must be an expression of the artist's
longings, passions and ideals. The art of music was rich in
potential genius when Beethoven died in 1827: Mendelssohn,
Chopin, Schumann and Liszt were youths of about 17, with
Wagner and Verdi following only three years behind. But in
France a lone romantic fire was already burning. Berlioz
was 24 when first inspired by the music of Beethoven, within
one year of the master's death, and was a self-conscious
prophet for the musical part of a literary and artistic revolution then erupting in Paris under the banner of Romanticism.

Romantic ideas and attitudes were born well back in the
18th century, with philosophic roots in the thought of Burke,
Rousseau, Herder and Kant. But despite pre-romantic literary
stirrings in England and the vigorous *Sturm und Drang* episode
in Germany during the 1770s and 80s, the new outlook only
became widespread at the turn of the century. As the old
order crumbled beneath the impact of political upheaval
from the French Revolution and from the first social effects
of the Industrial Revolution, there was an opportunity and
an incentive to construct a fresh inner world, even if bold
new notions like the Rights of Man had already become
obscured in the outer world. Paradoxically, it was in revolutionary France that the spread of romantic ideas was longest
delayed: an intolerant dictatorship and a rigid neoclassicism
in literature and the arts limited the initial influence of
important figures like Chateaubriand, Senancour and Mme.
de Staël, and the Romantic Movement remained largely
dormant until the 1820s.

But war failed to suppress the upsurging romantic faith
of key figures such as Novalis, Schelling and the Schlegel
brothers in Germany, or Wordsworth, Coleridge and Blake
in England. Later, as the works of Scott, Goethe, Byron
and others became widely available in translation — and also
Shakespeare and Dante from an earlier age — the pioneers
were joined by an eager post-war generation and the
intellectual and literary life of a whole continent was astir.
A new mode of personal expression burst from the shifting
social fabric of post-Napoleonic Europe, and in music this
romantic *avant garde* was led by Berlioz.

Creative man became a different creature as his rôle

evolved from that of a modest craftsman patronised by aristocrats into a self-conscious 'artist' with only a precarious economic foothold in the new bourgeois society. This change saw the birth of the modern notion of artists who starve in garrets, like the eccentric idealists of Puccini's *La Bohème*: painter, poet, philosopher and musician scraping a living in the Paris that Berlioz knew so well in the 1830s. In this hard and insecure world Romanticism provided a set of attitudes as an ideological prop, and artists emerged whose concerns about the meaning of existence and the nature of their own creativity were more truly part of their being than had been usual in the previous, more elegant century.

The exception was Beethoven, a product of the 18th century who became an exemplar for the new type of artist by sheer will-power as much as by economic circumstance. He was the first composer whose feelings about God and man were intense enough for us to hear them bursting the seams of his music, and whose dreams are themselves part of his art. He believed in what he called an 'empire of the mind', a concept to which Berlioz also subscribed in his own fashion. They were both the sort of lone, pioneering characters whose art, so they believed, could or would eventually re-shape the world. In its turn, the world has come to feel that in the face of such energy and conviction, artistic creations will be better understood if we know their creators. Thus music-lovers delve perennially into the details of composers' lives and personalities, often gaining useful insights, but as frequently meeting a baffling barrier between life and art.

It has been said that music is the smile upon the face of thought, which suggests a rather different path for exploration when seeking the non-musical roots of this elusive, abstract, but supremely expressive art. If 'thought' be interpreted generously to encompass the whole gamut of mental processes extending from cold logic to passionate feeling, especially as applied to those areas of attention not demanded by the hum-drum world of daily existence, we can find another, perhaps more exciting set of indices to illuminate the inspirations behind a composer's music. Apart from some unconventional speculations offered in an appendix, such illumination will not depend upon the highly conjectural art of posthumous psycho-analysis, but on Berlioz's known or reasonably surmised conscious beliefs and opinions, whether or not overtly connected with music.

Hopefully, the investigation will also be of interest in its own right and could help in the understanding of an epoch, or even a whole culture. Ideas, like lives, have their own impetus and identity, and when the mind of one man is considered within its cultural framework — rather as conventional biographies are set within history — a fascinating new world opens up. Properly speaking this world of ideas is part of history itself, a fact acknowledged by Carlyle when he asked in his essay *On History*: "what is all knowledge too but recorded experience, and a product of history; of which, therefore, reasoning and belief, no less than action and passion, are essential materials?"

There is a French concept *chant intérieur*, the ceaseless flow of music said to run through the minds of some composers and an object of great critical conjecture. In this study the equivalent of this 'internal song' will be those speculations on God, life, art, good and evil, the nature of man, and similar large questions, which can be deduced from the utterances and writings of one highly articulate composer. Berlioz had an ordered view of the world and expressed himself on many topics in a lively written style; he is thus richly revealing of his own mind. His *Memoirs* also happen to be one of the world's great autobiographies and should be read by all concerned about the place of art in society, or by anyone who wishes to savour a splendid and unique synthesis of rational argument and romantic ardour.

Berlioz was also the first composer whose every major work has a literary, historical or liturgical connection, even when purely instrumental in construction. Although in several instances this connection comprises no more than a title, Berlioz's need to offer such a link to his audience was both central to his outlook and to some extent symptomatic of the whole romantic ethos. Thus it is no accident that there are only two works in his whole musical output (academic exercises apart) without programmatic titles, the *Toccata* for harmonium and *Reverie and Caprice* for violin and orchestra — and one of these still hints at romantic moods. This is not to suggest that Berlioz's music has no aesthetic validity of its own, only to note that its aurally entrancing and often nobly beautiful structures can become even more exciting when we allow them to be inhabited by characters or ideas of the composer's own choosing.

Like his music, the framework of Berlioz's mind resembles a temple with a classically clean and balanced architecture, designed to house a drama of romantic passions. He said of himself that "it is in my nature to feel very intensely and at the same time . . . to see very clearly and steadily; but my true affections are immeasurably strong, and constant even to the edge of doom".[1] Thus by his own confession he was both rational and romantic, hence the title of this study.

When commending Jacques Barzun's massive and endlessly instructive book *Berlioz and the Romantic Century*, W.H. Auden said that "In order to understand the nineteenth century it is essential to understand Berlioz". After considering the interplay of reason, romance, and a host of other influences within Berlioz's mind — and his setting within a turbulent culture which became half our own inheritance — the reader may join the present author in feeling that in understanding the psyche of Hector Berlioz we become not only more appreciative of the last century (and of his music), but also gain a more balanced view of our own tangled age.

1

Casting the Spiritual Mould

Louis Hector Berlioz was born in France in 1803, at a time when Beethoven was putting the finishing touches to the *Eroica Symphony* in Vienna. In the world of music, Glinka and Bellini were the only men of note born within five years of Berlioz, but in other spheres his generation proved to be rich in genius. His contemporaries (1798 – 1808) included Balzac, Comte, Daumier, Delacroix, Disraeli, Dumas, Emerson, Garibaldi, Hugo, Longfellow, Mazzini, J.S. Mill, Pushkin, Saint-Beuve and George Sand; and if we add another year these are joined by Heine, Schubert and de Vigny in 1797 and by Darwin, Gladstone, Gogol, Lincoln, Mendelssohn, Poe and Tennyson in 1809.

While Berlioz was in his cradle, Lamarck laid the foundations of systematic biology and Chateaubriand's speculations seemed to promise a new Christianity; the first commercially viable steam-powered boat had just been launched and the first food-bottling factory opened; Herder and Kant died, leaving behind a whole school of philosophers to shape the thought of a century; war had recently re-started in Europe and the British army adopted the Shrapnel shell; as First Consul, Napoleon had dissolved a class of the Institut in Paris which studied social, psychological and philosophic matters from a liberal-Idéologue standpoint, and he was crowned Emperor of the French within a year. Such was the wider setting, which eventually shaped the composer's life and mind but which probably sent no more than the smallest ripples into the remoter parts of rural France in 1803.

Berlioz, son of a loving, well-read, humane man of medicine

and a conventional but somewhat over-pious mother, was born and grew up in La Côte Saint-André. This is a small town in the department of Isère in south-east France, situated between Lyons and Grenoble and not far from Vienne, an ancient town on the River Rhône. The beauty of this region had a lasting effect upon the young Berlioz, who always returned with gratitude and love to his birthplace and to his grandfather's village of Meylan, poised on a hillside just beyond Grenoble and looking across the Isère valley to the Dauphiné mountains. On the opening pages of his *Memoirs*, written when he was 44, Berlioz describes the setting of his boyhood home:

> It overlooks a wide, rich plain, green and golden and in its stillness filled with a sense of dreamlike grandeur — a grandeur enhanced by the chain of mountains bounding the plain to the south and east, behind which, far off, gleaming with glaciers, rise the towering peaks of the Alps.[2]

Love of nature was joined by the urge to know about exotic far-away places. Poring over his father's maps and books, particularly Bougainville's *Voyage Round the World*, he developed a passion for the idea of travel and was fascinated by the customs of strange peoples and the geography of distant lands — particularly the South Sea Islands. Although he never travelled outside Europe, this obsession persisted into middle age, by which time a taste for the scenic and the exotic had become an accepted part of romantic culture, and we find him so agitated by the prospect of his own son going to sea that only intense musical activity enables him to keep his presence of mind:

> This ardent occupation [with musical projects] is the only one that can help me to repress a growing love of travel. I dream only of ships, seas, distant isles, adventurous explorations. My musical voyagings through Europe have only developed this half-buried instinct of old. I can see its futility, its childishness, but can do nothing about it.[3]

Boyhood education came mainly from his father, for whose patient and persevering efforts Berlioz remained ever grateful. But eventually he came to realise that in missing the rough and tumble of school in later boyhood he had retained a certain shyness and naïvity, against which his more extravagant romantic poses may be seen as a reaction. At first he did not take readily to poetry or the classics, but gradually the power of great literature overtook him, especially the epic passages of Virgil which he mastered in the original Latin. It seems that he retained sufficient knowledge of this language to converse in it when necessary during his travels in later life, and even felt confident enough to chide those who (according to him) mispronounced the ancient tongue. About a quarter of all the many literary quotations in his letters are in Latin, chiefly from Virgil. On one occasion, when reciting to his father the death of Dido from the *Aeneid*, Hector was quite overcome with emotion: "I rushed away, out of sight of everybody, to indulge my Virgilian grief".[4] This was the beginning of a fifty-year passion which led finally to his opera *The Trojans*.

Later he developed similar passions for Byron, Schiller, Goethe, Hugo, Moore and, above all, Shakespeare, whom he revered with Beethoven as a demi-god. But we anticipate. While still a child he underwent a trinity of deep emotional experiences involving love, music and religion — all at around the age of twelve and all to have a profound and lasting influence on his spiritual condition. Love came in the figure of Estelle, a girl six years his senior whose very name was geared to evoke deep feelings in the boy who had secretly devoured Florian's pastoral romance *Estelle et Némorin*. The setting, also, was auspicious, for the mountainside house high up in Meylan in which this real Estelle resided was, Berlioz notes, "half hidden in gardens and vineyards with a wide prospect over the valley of the Isère far below; behind, a few craggy hillocks, an old tower in ruins, a wood, and the commanding bulk of the great rock-bastion of Saint-Eynard: in fact a spot clearly marked out to be the scene of some romantic drama".[5] That drama was instant:

> The moment I beheld her, I was conscious of an electric shock: I loved her. From then on I lived in a daze. I hoped for nothing, I knew nothing, and yet my heart felt weighed down by an immense sadness. I lay awake whole nights disconsolate. By day I hid myself in the maize fields or in the secret corners of my grandfather's orchard, like a wounded bird, mute, suffering. . . . Everyone at home and in the neighbourhood laughed at the spectacle of a child of twelve broken on the wheel of a love beyond his years . . . . Time is powerless. No other loves can efface the imprint of this first love.[6]

Here speaks the true romantic, caught forever in the web of an ideal but impossible attachment, and always thereafter seeking some equivalent inspiration. So, through two marriages and various love affairs, leading back late in life to a meeting with Estelle as a kind but uncomprehending old lady, Berlioz carried deep in his psyche the notion of perfect love, which he often equated with art and which indeed profoundly influenced his choice of subjects for musical expression. "There are many sorts of love", said Berlioz to a friend:

> The kind I feel is the true, grand, poetic love. I have known it since the first time and nothing is more beautiful. With the love of art, there is no other divinizing of the human heart. With it the world grows bright, horizons enlarge, all nature takes on colour and vibrates in endless harmonies, and — one loves, that's all, one loves: [7]

The two other firmly implanted influences were aspects of a single event — also very much concerned with 'divinizing of the human heart'. Although he had commenced musical studies with flute and guitar during the previous year, Berlioz had his first important musical *experience* at a religious ceremony: first communion, taken at an Ursuline convent where his elder sister was a boarder.

> Deeply moved, I crossed the threshold of the chapel. I found myself in the midst of a multitude of young girls in white, my sister's friends; and with them I knelt in prayer and waited for the solemn ceremony to begin. . . . . . . I received the sacrament. As I did so, a chorus of fresh young voices broke into the eucharistic hymn. The sound filled me with a kind of mystical, passionate unrest which I was powerless to hide . . . . . . I saw Heaven open — a Heaven of love and pure delight, purer and a thousand times lovelier than the one that had so often been described to me. Such is the magic power of true expression, the incomparable beauty of melody that comes from the heart. [8]

Thus art and religion were united in a ceremonial drama, a coupling to which Berlioz repeatedly returned in his music and came eventually to regard as the supreme expression of artistic faith. Despite his childhood beliefs, this faith did not incorporate the Catholic dogmas (or any specifically Christian theology), but did draw on a fund of religious feeling in the general sense, and attached enormous value to deeply felt musical occasions organised in a ceremonial fashion.

The boyhood roots of Berlioz's mind may now be sum-
marised under six headings: love of nature and the idea of
travel; a capacity for intense romantic love; a growing appreciation of literature and poetry; deep religious feelings,
channelled towards the church by a devout mother; wide
general interests and liberality of outlook, in emulation of a
kindly, rationalistic father; and a growing passion for music
as the expressive art *par excellence*. In all essentials the
spiritual mould had been cast by the time he left home in
1821.

Berlioz was not quite eighteen when he went to Paris, in
theory to study medicine, in practice to be finally engulfed
by music and the desire to become a composer. The dissecting
room horrified him, but the scientific parts of his medical
studies left their mark on his mind and no doubt contributed
to the breadth of interests and articulate sharpness of critical
faculty that persisted through his life. Also, as is common
when young men come together in a great city for university
studies, he was swept along by political and social movements
which played their part in shaping his later attitudes.

The story of Berlioz's disagreement with his family over
the move from medicine to music, and the ensuing long
struggle for admission to the Conservatoire; the further four
years of composition and study before obtaining the much
coveted *Prix de Rome*; his extraordinary passion-at-a-distance
for the Anglo-Irish actress Harriet Smithson, and the part this
played in the composition of the *Fantastic Symphony*; his
love affair with, engagement to and subsequent attempted
suicide over Camille Moke; his stay in Italy and eventual
marriage to Harriet; all these may be studied at depth in
various biographies and in Berlioz's own *Memoirs*. Throughout this period, and more germane to our thesis, his personality grew to make multifarious contact with the intellectual,
social and artistic life around him, and from these meeting-
points, new ideas, attitudes and devotions were shaped in his
mind. The social-economic reformism of Saint-Simon mingled
with vague yearnings for a Napoleonic heroism which had
been part of the political climate in his childhood. A Voltair-
ean scepticism, partly inherited from his father, eroded his
Christian faith. Above all, he worshipped the great creators —
composers, writers and artists — championed their work and
came to detest both the academic conservatism which stifles

experiment and the philistinism which prefers to be entertained rather than exalted.

In one sense Berlioz's long fight for musical recognition in
his own country, his "Thirty Years' War against the routineers,
the professors, and the deaf",[9] is in itself a biography of the
man's mind. If in the pursuit of his religious, philosophic,
ethical and political evolution we seem to cross and re-cross
an ever-present battlefield labelled Artistic Idealism v. Philistinism, this is simply because the tactics and strategy of this
battle were seldom far from the consciousness of Hector
Berlioz. Despite recurrent bouts of pessimism and what he
called the 'disease of isolation', his principal faith was in the
ultimate sanctity of great art, and his most persistent fear was
of the brutish, herd instincts in men which denied this vision.
Assessment of the strength or weakness of this, Berlioz's
personal *idée fixe*, must await our final pages.

2

Disbelieving Rationalist

We have seen how at the age of twelve Berlioz was profoundly impressed by ceremonial beauty as revealed in the
Roman Catholic liturgy. His reaction was such that:

> This charming religion (so attractive since it gave up burning people*)
> was for seven whole years the joy of my life, and although we have long
> since fallen out, I have always kept most tender memories of it . . . at
> a blow, I became a saint — such a saint that I attended Mass every day
> and took communion every Sunday, and went regularly to confession
> in order to say to my director 'Father, I have done nothing.'[10]

The end of this saintly seven-year period saw him in Paris,
where his Christian beliefs were quickly shattered. The
emphasis here is on beliefs rather than feelings because
Berlioz seemed to retain right until the end of his life some
capacity for religious feeling and expression — some yearning
of the soul for meaning and hope in an apparently impersonal
and very material universe. But this was sentiment, not
theology, and he was well aware that in rejecting dogmas
uncongenial to his intellect while still seeking something
worthy of worship in nature or in art, his spirit must be
forever discontented.

Neither an atheist in the narrow materialist sense, nor able
to accept God in either theistic or deistic guise, Berlioz could
have 'passionate interviews' with nature and praise its human
disciples ecstatically, yet feel himself "tugged at in the
opposite direction by an analytic mania which the — so to

*The year 1781 saw the Inquisition's last victim to die at the stake.

speak — chemical philosophy of our time breeds in the brain".[11] In this chapter we shall explore this 'chemical philosophy', the negative aspect of Berlioz's religious outlook, and then see in the next chapter to what extent the void was filled with worship of different kinds: feelings in place of faith.

Berlioz, always a humorist, a man of laughter, often poked simple irreverent fun at God and the church. He relates a delightful episode with Mendelssohn in Rome in 1831:

> As I was propounding some outrageous thesis or other in answer to the strictly orthodox and pious views put forward by him, his foot slipped and the next moment he was lying in a bruised condition at the bottom of a steep ruined staircase. 'Look at that for an example of divine justice' I said, helping him on to his feet. 'I blaspheme, you fall'.[12]

Mendelssohn was deeply offended and they never discussed religion again. Berlioz frequently concocted light-hearted but technically blasphemous analogies, such as: ". . . like the good Lord and other scoundrels";[13] or, referring to a triangle, "Its shape is in the image of God, like all triangles, but more than other triangles, and more than God in particular, you will find it plays true";[14] or "The Pope is a barbarian, like most other sovereigns".[15] He was also inclined to be contemptuous of clerics in the lower orders, as when he found them in abundance in the Rome of 1831:

> These abbés, monks, priests are everywhere, right and left, above, below, within, without, with the poor and the rich in church, at dances and cafés, in the theatres, with the ladies in cabriolets, on foot with the men . . . Everywhere.[16]

In similar mocking vein, Berlioz wrote of Henry VIII: "this good king used to come in to give thanks to God and sing some hallelujas of his own composition every time he had invented a new religion or beheaded one of his wives".[17] More sardonic is a piece of fiction — or perhaps some real experience transmuted into a parable about the sort of religious music that Berlioz always disliked:

> The programme consists of an enormous oratorio, which the public goes to hear as a matter of religious duty, to which it listens in religious silence, which the artists endure with religious fortitude,

and which engenders in everybody a chilling boredom, black and thick as the walls of a Protestant church.[18]

This hints at another aspect of Berlioz's irreligion — his dislike of Protestantism in general and Puritanism in particular. In the passage from the *Memoirs* where he refers to 'tender memories' of the Roman faith despite his apostasy, he says also that such was its appeal for him that if he had "had the misfortune to be born into the bosom of one of those schisms ponderously hatched by Luther or Calvin, I would undoubtedly have abjured it the moment I was able, and flung myself into the arms of the fair Roman at the earliest promptings of poetic instinct".[19] Note the reason given, 'poetic instinct' not doctrine. This perhaps illuminates a suggestion by the German poet Heinrich Heine (exiled in Paris and a friend of Berlioz) that the many Romantics who turned to Rome as the nineteenth century progressed, did so because they were pantheists at heart, Catholicism being a pantheistic faith.

Discussing possible operatic subjects in 1839 with the librettist Eugène Scribe, Berlioz mentioned that "certain individuals and periods are deeply uncongenial to me — Luther, for example, the Christians of the Lower Empire and those boorish Druids".[20] It seems that Luther epitomised for Berlioz an intolerant puritanism and the sort of Old Testament faith that leads to religious wars. In a letter describing musical activities in Prague in 1846 he digresses substantially from the task in hand in order to vent his feelings about certain types of protestant choral society, and, barely disguised, about their religion:

These meeting houses of musical puritanism are the repositories of the religion not of the beautiful, whatever its age, but of the old whatever the quality: a narrow, rancorous religion with its Bible and the works of two or three evangelists, over which the faithful pore tirelessly, producing ever more subtle interpretations of passages whose meaning is transparently clear, finding deep and mystical conceptions where the rest of the world sees only savagery and barbarism, and always ready with a Hosanna even when the God of Moses commands them to 'take the infants and dash them against the stones, and give the blood thereof for dogs to lick, and not suffer their eyes to pity them'. So beware of these bigots! They would drive a sane man into forgetting the respect and admiration due to the great achievements of the past.[21]

Here, Berlioz is driven towards atheism by feelings of moral revulsion, which also seems to have been the case when he inscribed his copy of Bernardin de Saint-Pierre's popular story *Paul et Virginie* with a note to the effect that the tale would convert the reader to atheism were he not already of that persuasion. Curiously, the book's prime moral, following the teachings of Rousseau, was that suffering is unavoidable when man turns his back on the simple life of nature. But it must have had many meanings for its vast readership. Even the somewhat philistine Bonaparte found it so moving that he pensioned and decorated the author, who died in the year of Napoleon's banishment to Elba. Saint-Pierre would probably have been surprised that anyone should deduce atheism from his writings. He was a deist who favoured a psychology based on positive sentiments rather than on an interplay of neutral sensations, the latter derived from Locke via Condillac and favoured by the Idéologue school of thought which he disliked.

This suggests that Berlioz as a young man was predisposed to justify a secular outlook wherever he could. Certainly his negative pronouncements on religion — when not simply witty — were usually expressions of genuine intellectual doubt or simple hints of disbelief. When not devouring Shakespeare, Goethe, *et al*, he was inclined to study works with a philosophically radical bias, finding to his dismay in Italy in 1831 that most of the literature he admired was on the Papal Index. And when the forbidden fruits were to hand he sometimes saw further than the authors (or their censors) would dare to look, as when he criticised the philosopher-physicians Cabanis and Gall for refusing to draw logical conclusions from their arguments for fear of an adverse public reaction, the missing conclusions again being atheistic. The Frenchman Georges Cabanis, who died when Berlioz was a boy but whose writings were preserved on his father's book-shelves, came to be regarded as the scientific vindicator of the Idéologues' analytical psychology. He was a detached agnostic for most of his life and founded the physiologically based psychology which led more than a century later to Pavlov and thence to modern behaviourism. Franz Gall, a German of the same age and similar interests, survived for twenty years more to pioneer the now rather suspect pseudo-science of phrenology.

In a letter expressing agreement with the political and social aims of Saint-Simonism (see page 43), Berlioz felt a need to qualify his support: "but I must tell you that my notions have not changed a bit as regards views of the super-human, God, the soul, and the life beyond".[22] There was a nominal religious element in the later doctrines of Saint-Simon as expounded in his *New Christianity* — and as developed by some of his disciples under Prosper Enfantin, who founded an eccentric sacerdotal community and practised a 'religion of love' (including free-love). But Saint-Simon's central thesis was ethical and social, incorporated no theology, and had evolved from a distinctly positivist/scientific position (Auguste Comte, founder of Positivism, worked with Saint-Simon for a while). Thus it was hardly necessary for a would-be disciple of sceptical bend to make a special declaration of his theological position unless he felt strongly on the matter.

That he held negative views on dogmatic or doctrinal aspects of Christianity is also evidenced by a note in the second chapter of the *Memoirs*. Here he expresses loving wonder at his own father's willingness to bend over backwards in keeping a promise to Mme. Berlioz that he would not interfere with the inculcation of a faith in which he did not believe, but which she regarded as essential for her son's salvation. "On several occasions, I remember, he went so far as to hear my catechism — evidence of a degree of scrupulousness or philosophical impartiality of which I confess I should be incapable were my own son concerned".[23] It is interesting to note that the poet and playwright Alfred de Vigny, a leading romantic figure and even more defiantly anti-theistic than Berlioz, was also the product of a devout mother and free-thinking father. He shared Berlioz's spiritual loneliness and his eventual stoicism — and they were friends.

Writing to Liszt in 1834, Berlioz quotes some lines from one of Thomas Moore's *Sacred Songs*, which end: 'There's nothing bright but heaven'. He goes on: "But I do not believe in heaven. It is horrible to confess it. My heaven is the poetic world and there is a slug on each blossom".[24] Despite many radiant artistic blossoms, the slugs of pessimism persisted for Berlioz, never to be expunged by the religious faith to which Liszt returned from time to time. In later life Berlioz corresponded at length with the Princess Carolyne Sayn-Wittgen-stein, Liszt's mistress/companion, and in an off-quoted letter

to her said: "like you I have one of the three theological
virtues — charity — but not, as you know, the other two."[25]
Thus faith and hope were to elude him, at least in their
theological sense, though at times an aggressive disbelief gave
way to a gentle, questing agnosticism — a tendency to regard
the deity and human existence as insoluble enigmas rather
than matters for firm and final definition either by faith or
reason. Thus in another letter to the Princess he equates
theological disputes with the clash of "arbitrary systems
designed to forward a special cause",[26] and in his *Memoirs*
he follows an emotional passage on his sister's suffering and
death with the declaration:

> How meaningless are all those questions of faith, free will, the exist-
> ence of God, and the rest of it; an endless maze in which man's
> baffled understanding wanders hopelessly lost.[27]

3

A Religion of Feeling

The rationalist and sceptical elements in Berlioz's religious outlook were indeed only elements, intellectual polarities balanced by emotional opposites and diluted in his own special brand of romantic religion — worship of the beautiful in nature and in art. Berlioz was easily moved by the grandeur of nature and anxious that audiences should know of its effect on his music. Thus in 1855 he prescribed the contents of an autobiographical note, pointing out the great "influence of the spectacle of nature, which will be found reflected in the Adagio of *Romeo and Juliet*, the Scenes in the Country of the *Fantastic Symphony*, and the Serenade and Pilgrim's March of *Harold in Italy*".[28] However, the inspiration was not direct, for in the same year he wrote in envy to Wagner, saying: "It must be wonderful to be able to write in the presence of grand scenery! . . . . Alas! Such joy is denied me! Beautiful country, towering peaks, a turbulent sea absorb me completely, instead of exciting me to thought. I feel but cannot express myself. I am only able to paint the moon when seeing its image at the bottom of a well".[29] But he was grateful for the balm of such interludes:

> What marvellous sunsets, what peace on those heights and what purity in that layer of the atmosphere! Only such passionate interviews with nature as these can make me forget for an instant the griefs of outraged love or art. But these very same sights quickly kindle them again more burning than before: all is inter-linked.[30]

More specifically religious, but linked with his attitude to nature, are his feelings about the Rogation ceremony.

Commenting on his first childhood experience of the sense of
isolation and despair which plagued him at intervals throughout his life, he records how his thoughts were interrupted by
a passing procession chanting a prayer, rather in the manner
of the Easter procession which he used to interrupt Faust's
suicidal reverie in *The Damnation of Faust* (Goethe used a
Choir of Angels): "There is to me something poetic and
inexpressibly moving in this traditional visitation of the
fields in spring to ask for Heaven's blessing on the fruits of
the earth".[31] Thus Berlioz acknowledges the mystery — perhaps the miracle — of life and growth: biological nature. The
sterner stuff of geological nature, the majestic but indifferent
rocks, mountains and oceans, brought forth from Berlioz a
magnificent pantheistic invocation — also in the *Damnation*:

> Nature, dread, unfathomable, alone,
> Only you give pause to my unending ennui,
> On your omnipotent breast I feel my misery less keenly,
> I regain my strength, and believe in life at last.
> Yes, blow, you hurricanes! Roar, you mighty forests!
> Crash down, you rocks, and torrents, hurl headlong your waters!
> My voice delights to mingle with your majestic sounds.
> Forests, rocks, torrents, I worship you.
> Glittering worlds above, to you the longing
> Of a heart too vast and a soul insatiable cries out
> For the happiness it cannot seize.

Here is man crying out to the Universe for a spiritual satis-
faction not found on Earth for more than fleeting moments.
In the sixteen years that had passed since Berlioz first responded to Goethe's version of the story with his *Eight Scenes
from Faust* (in which Faust himself did not appear), a matur-
ing and complex blend of romantic aspiration and worldly
frustration had made it possible for him to identify with the
drama's central character — to share some of his hopes and
much of his agonised loneliness. Perhaps that is why, when he
returned to the theme in 1846, now confident enough in his
literary powers to write some of the libretto without assistance, it was this very passage that he tackled first. The words
he chose seem to represent more of himself than Goethe, an
impression underlined by a parallel declaration in a letter
written two years later. After some gloomy reflections on
the frustrations he had suffered in France "because the

national mentality is stupid where serious matters of art and literature are concerned", he continues as follows:

> Like a savage I go my own way, I hold on to my freedom, I keep moving as long as the earth will bear me, as long as the woods have moose and deer: and if I am often weary and sleepless and suffer from cold, hunger and the ravages of the pale-faces, at least I can dream alone above the waterfall and in the silent forest, worshipping the grandeur of nature and thanking God that He has left me a feeling for her beauty.[32]

Here, bathed in a Rousseau-like wash of liberty set in North American surroundings resembling those found in Chateaubriand's *René* and *Atala* — twin stories well known to Berlioz — the sceptic actually thanks God for granting some amelioration of his condition. Paralleling this, a good deal of religious assuagement is also to be found in his music, a fact which has caused much speculation and puzzlement amongst Berlioz's biographers and critics. Indeed, because of his various atheistic declarations — and particularly because of the pictorial, dramatic and noisy manner in which he depicts the day of judgement in the *Requiem* and parodies the *Dies Irae* theme in the disrespectful witches brew of the *Fantastic Symphony*'s finale — it has often been assumed that his sole reason for choosing religious subjects was their dramatic fitness for his music. This view no doubt contains a large element of truth, while perhaps overlooking the all-embracing or Shakespearian nature of Berlioz's view of the human condition, wherein the extremes of terror, delicate love, worship, rough humour, sadness, lone mysticism, exultations and death, all join hands — and lead one to speculate on the meaning of things.

His temperamental bias here is revealed in a comment on Lamartine, poet of Byronic melancholy who tended to pursue the 'infinite' even when dabbling in revolutionary politics: "Oh! he is a great poet! What a pity he is so incomplete! He never leaves the skies; nevertheless a poet should be a mirror in which all objects, gracious and horrible, brilliant and sombre, calm and agitated, are reflected".[33] It so happened that despite his literary craft, Lamartine believed the poetry of music to be more nearly the language of the infinite — more Godlike — than the poetry of words, and even went so far as to say that if he had the chance of a second life he would choose to be a musical genius. He would therefore probably have reversed Berlioz's judgement, and approved the fact that the composer's first sizeable work was, so to say, set in the sky. This was the Mass of 1825, from which only the *Resurrexit* now survives.

This was but a preliminary musical skirmish with the Catholic liturgy, and Berlioz tells us, in connection with his commission twelve years later to compose the full *Requiem*, that

> the text of the Requiem was a quarry that I had long coveted. Now at last it was mine, and I fell upon it with a kind of fury. My brain felt as though it would explode with the pressure of ideas.[34]

Much of the 'explosion' in the resulting *Grande Messe des Morts* is of course purely musico-dramatic, though it should not be forgotten that the first performance was given and accepted as a liturgical event and moved devout Catholics to tears. Even today, non-Christians prepared to practise Coleridge's "willing suspension of disbelief for the moment, which constitutes poetic faith" may be moved in a religious manner by the *Sanctus* or by the wonderfully ethereal *Amen* — perhaps also by the thrilling upward sweep of violins occurring at the word *luceat* (light) just before the *Kyrie* and again near the end of the *Agnus Dei*. Those two inspired moments might even have symbolised the well remembered glow of mystical light which enveloped the young Berlioz at his first Communion. But here the borderline between musical and mystical experience is ill-defined, and Berlioz himself may simply have suspended his disbelief while composing, just as we all allow imagination to overrule the frequent mechanical and psychological absurdities of opera in the theatre.

Apart from the *Requiem* and *Te Deum*, ostensibly proclamations of Catholic faith, nearly all of Berlioz's major works contain *religioso* passages or movements which the composer felt to be inspired by religious feelings. Possibly this was for him sometimes simply a name for certain types of musical expression, though it is difficult, for instance, to feel that the composer of *Romeo and Juliet* did not believe in the type of humanitarian Christianity propounded by Friar Laurence in the finale. Other departures from Shakespeare's story in this work may be explained by reference to Garrick's version, commonly performed well into the 19th century and taken

to Paris by Charles Kemble's company in 1827 to provide
Berlioz with his shattering first experience of Shakespeare.
But the finale, expanding as it does the role of Friar Laurence
to provide a moving sermon and a great oath of reconciliation,
is almost pure Berlioz — albeit versified for the composer
by his friend Emile Deschamps.

In the play there is no sermon, merely a brief admonition
from the Prince ('See, what a scourge is laid upon your hate,/
That heaven finds means to kill your joys with love'), while
Montague and Capulet relent almost as briefly. Yet Berlioz,
despite his intense dislike of those who meddle with works of
art — and who made a particular point of castigating composers for "grotesque libretti called operas"[35] on this very
play — actually praised Garrick for allowing Juliet to awake
before Romeo had died, and represented the episode orches-
trally (Tomb Scene) in some of the most adventurous and
forward-looking music he ever penned. Also, he deemed it
permissible to create an entirely new vocal finale for his
symphonic version of the story — an ending clearly religious
in tone, in a manner not to be found in Shakespeare. Chastis-
ing the noisy crowds who would have vengeance, the Friar
speaks:

> Silence, you wretches! How can you without compunction
> In the face of so much love show so much hate?
> . . . .
> God, with a spark of Thy fire
> Touch these hard and sullen hearts;
> And may the breath of Thy wisdom,
> Breathing on them at my words,
> Scatter their anger
> Like chaff before the wind.
>
> Swear, then, by this dread symbol,
> . . . .
> Swear all of you, swear by the Holy Cross
> To affix between you a perpetual chain
> of holy charity and brotherly love;
> And God who holds in His hands the judgement of the world
> In the book of forgiveness will inscribe this oath.

It seems improbable that Berlioz could have created these
words and their music solely to produce a rousing finale.

Shakespeare's story was, after all, practically an object of worship for him, suggesting that he really intended audiences to follow his feelings into an area of sanctity — to believe in and to share the sentiments of Friar Laurence. He might also have been influenced by Weber's *Der Freischutz*, which features an old hermit who commends religious forgiveness just before the opera's finale. His deep love of this work, which draws on the dark Romanticism of the German forests and which he produced for the Opéra two years later, could have played a part in the creation of his own trans-Shakespearean holy man.

Whatever their genesis, the Friar's words ring with sincerity, as do many passages in *The Infant Christ* (the common literal translation 'The Childhood of Christ' is misleading) which have a touching simplicity glowing with religious feeling. While some critics have suggested that this is due merely to the universality of a simple human story, the archetypal nature of such a story can, by its very symbolism, have religious significance. It happens that Berlioz was very specific over his feelings about this work, saying of the finale "in that vocal peroration the whole work is summed up, for it seems to me that the feeling of the infinite, of divine love, is in that passage".[36] Likewise after a successful performance to a vast audience in Germany: "I am back .... ground to powder, deeply moved .... you cannot imagine the effect of the final mystic chorus: it was the religious ecstasy which I had dreamed of and felt in composing it".[37]

This was a work produced in middle age; but twenty years earlier, when in Rome, Berlioz had shown himself capable of devout feeling with his fine *Religious Meditation*. Ironically, this was a setting of the very Thomas Moore poem (second of the *Sacred Songs*) which had prompted him to declare to Liszt his disbelief in heaven quoted in the previous chapter. Thus are rationalism and religion found coexisting in one mind; a common enough paradox perhaps, but particularly evident amongst the Romantics, who exposed personal feelings to an unprecedented public glare which has made it easier for later generations to accept logic and intuition as uneasy but very human partners.

The romantic expression of what he regarded as religious feelings was for Berlioz necessarily a communal matter, an activity for art and ceremony in which many hearts are moved together. His initial emotional conviction on these lines came, as we saw, at his first communion, and was confirmed within a few years when he read Chateaubriand's *Spirit of Christianity* (Génie du Christiaisme). Francois-René de Chateaubriand, soldier, poet, traveller, novelist, diplomat, philosopher and popular theologian, a romantic monarchist at heart but infinitely adaptable in a revolutionary world, was a prime influence in the emergence of Romanticism in France. His book on Christianity — which originally included the novelette *René* that joined *Atala* in shaping Berlioz's 'lonely' type of romanticism — appeared a year before the composer's birth and was regarded at the time as a literary celebration of the recent Franco/Papal Concordat. Despite Napoleon's general distaste for unconventional or overtly romantic ideas, a sentimental streak in the First Consul prompted him to order official readings from Chateaubriand's book — which he no doubt found suitably uplifting as he dreamed of the time when Pope Pius VII would come to Paris to crown him Emperor. But although Chateaubriand was awarded a minor diplomatic post, he became estranged from Bonaparte in 1804 and his real period of influence was postponed until the post-war era, when France came late to Romanticism.

His book was in only the most superficial sense a theological work, being concerned more with a religion of feeling and the grandeur of the Church than with matters of doctrine, and thus providing an intellectual basis for the evolving romantic view of art as a quasi-religion. It was the ritualistic, humanist and aesthetic elements in Christianity that appealed to Berlioz, the 'poetic' factors more evident in Catholicism than in Protestantism. But while he was attracted by Chateaubriand's interest in the mysterious and secret forces which inspire creativity, it is unlikely that the sceptic within Berlioz would have agreed with his plea for religious belief on the grounds that "He who believes nothing is not far from believing everything; you have conjurors when you cease to have prophets, enchantments when you renounce religious ceremonies".[38]

While he chose a Roman framework on which to erect his religious music, he had no illusions that this gave his art a wider validity. Commenting on a suggestion that Mendelssohn's music lacked universality because of 'Hebraic elements', Berlioz asks: What kind of music is it that can ever become 'the property of the whole world, without distinction of time or place'? None, most certainly. The works of the great German masters such as Gluck, Haydn, Mozart and Beethoven, who all belonged to the Catholic — which is to say, 'universal' — religion, will no more achieve universality than the rest."[39] The forms of Catholicism just happened to match his poetic feelings; he felt rather than believed, and was able to express himself in music and ceremonies carrying labels which he could not take literally but whose presence he found relatively inoffensive.

His need for full and colourful expression led him to criticise a great deal of traditional religious music, whether meagre chants handed down for centuries under Rome, or vulgar hymns sung in gloomy churches under the influence of Calvin or Luther. But his battles with the philistines in this sphere were part of a wider campaign about musical expressiveness in general, and thus do not necessarily signify much in purely religious terms. However, his ideals for religious music (or a musical religion) were massive: in the imaginary future city of Euphonia described in *Evenings with the Orchestra* (25th evening) no effort is spared in promoting "noble use of all the resources of art in the divine service".[40]

The willingness to co-operate at a 'poetic' level with institutions whose dogmas he found unacceptable, is paralleled in Berlioz's personal relationships. If a companion's beliefs differed from his own he would try to avoid giving offence — the major exception to this being the Mendelssohn episode related earlier, which he came to regret. His lifelong friends Humbert Ferrand and Joseph d'Ortigue were devout Catholics, and Ferrand's religious convictions in particular made him an ardent opponent of the somewhat anti-clerical revolution of 1830. Berlioz supported the uprising, but their friendship survived. Indeed, less than two years later he sent Ferrand (who wrote poetry under the name of Georges Araudas) the outline of a story for a religious opera in the hope that he would produce a libretto.

The theme was Christ's second coming to bring Judgement to a rich but decadent world, with a vastly conceived final scene employing the sort of musical forces that were eventually used in the *Requiem* five years later. Nothing came of *The Last Day of the World*, but had it materialised one can imagine it creating just the sort of puzzlement that has arisen over the 'atheist's' handling of the liturgy in the Mass. That Berlioz was in fact unconvinced by the subject matter he proposed is evidenced in a letter he wrote to the composer/conductor Ferdinand Hiller at this time: "I am going to see Ferrand . . . . you see extremes meet. He is more religious than ever . . . . "[41] When Liszt took holy orders in 1865 Berlioz expressed the hope that this would give him some consolation and happiness — despite the fear voiced by Princess Sayn-Wittgenstein that he might poke irreverent fun.

Paradoxically, it was in the same spirit of rational impartiality coupled with a romantic respect for true religious feeling that he composed the *Amen* fugue from the *Damnation of Faust*, sung by a crowd of irreverent revellers in Auerbach's cellar. Berlioz was well aware that in prescribing a fast fugue for this famous parody on the word 'amen' he was simply following an established pattern often found in conventional religious music, a practice which, oddly enough, he regarded as indecently irreligious: "These traditional fugues are nothing but senseless blasphemy".[42] Thus when Mephistopheles remarks: "By heaven, gentlemen, your fugue is very fine; / to hear it / One would suppose one was in some holy place", Berlioz is really pulling everyone's leg, believers and unbelievers alike. This attitude is paralleled in the last movement of the *Fantastic Symphony*, where tolling bells followed by tubas or ophicleides playing the *Dies Irae* were meant to remind Paris audiences of the practice, then still extant in many churches, of employing serpents to play plainsong themes in alternation with choir and organ, producing a notoriously horrible noise. In his treatise on instrumentation (see Chapter 8) Berlioz refers to the serpent's "frigid and abominable blaring" but concedes its suitability for the awesome *Dies Irae* theme. So, was he attacking the Mass or its musical desecration when he used these sounds to introduce a Black Sabbath?

Further evidence of impartiality was his reaction to the charge that the music of Mendelssohn was somehow 'marred' by a Jewish influence, even though the composer was a lifelong Lutheran. Berlioz tackles the accusation with calm civility: "Is there not a little prejudice involved in this way of judging that great musician, and would M. de Lenz have written these lines if he had not known that the composer of *St. Paul* and *Elijah* was descended from the famous Jew

Moses Mendelssohn? I find it hard to believe".[43]

His incredulity commends itself to minds carrying the imprint of Hitler's extermination camps; but in the 1850s, long before French anti-Semitism exploded around the Dreyfus affair, a subtle 'anthropological' racialism came into vogue. This was given a wash of intellectual respectability by Joseph de Gobineau's *Essay on the Inequality of Human Races*, which appealed to Wagner, who had written his notorious *Judaism in Music* article not long before.[44] Berlioz's incorruptible detachment should be seen against this background — but this shifts the emphasis from religion to social ethics, and thus to another chapter.

4

Composer as Social Critic

She died of cancer of the breast after six months of frightful suffering which day and night made her cry out in agony . . . . . Yet no
doctor dared have the humanity to end it once and for all with a
little chloroform. They do it so as to spare patients the pain of an
operation which lasts a few seconds, but they will not consider
using it to save them six months of torture, when it is absolutely
certain that no remedy, not even time, will cure the disease, and
death is clearly the one remaining boon, the sole source of happiness. The law, however, is against it, and the doctrines of religion
are no less rigidly opposed. And my sister herself would no doubt
have rejected this way of escape if it had been offered to her. 'God's
will be done' — as if everything that happened were not God's will,
and as if God's will would not have been well manifested in the
release of the patient by a swift and peaceful death as in the pro-
longing of her senseless and abominable suffering.[45]

Thus Berlioz reacted to the death of his elder sister Nanci in
1850. Such a plea for euthanasia, apart from its lingering
concern for the theological implications, is positive advocacy
of moral change in the manner of Enlightenment rationalism —
and of course in the spirit of modern liberalism, which owes
much to the 18th century *philosophes*. This was the defiant,
reformist Berlioz, who at other times was hopelessly depress-
ed by human folly and contracted into a spiritual shell. His
last ten years were wrapped in personal tragedy: *The Trojans*
never received a proper performance; his younger sister
Adèle died, followed by his second wife Marie; he was plagued
with recurrent illness and long bouts of pain; then, less than

two years before his own death, his only son Louis died while abroad. He loved his son dearly, but never gave him the devoted attention in childhood which he had received from his own father — very much the reverse, in fact — thus adding an element of remorse to his despairing sadness at the loss. All was conducive to pessimism. In the letter to the Princess in which he denied two of the three theological virtues he makes the following declaration:

> The insoluble riddle of the world, the existence of evil and pain, the mad fury of the human race, its stupid ferocity, which it vents, everywhere and at all times, upon the most innocent people and often on itself, have reduced me to the state of spiritless and desperate resignation which may be supposed to exist in a scorpion surrounded by live coals.[46]

But the scorpion was not always surrounded and would sometimes spit back at a hostile world. Thus on 'arranged' marriages:

> When I see such stupid compliance and insolent parental requirements, such disgusting cruelty crushing out fine passions . . . . . I should like to be able to put all reasonable people, virtuous heroines, and far-sighted fathers into a sack with a hundred thousand pounds of good sense and throw them into the sea.[47]

Likewise in reaction to an execution offered, as was the custom, to the public as a gruesome 'highlight' of the Roman Carnival in 1831:

> some luckless bandit . . . . . taken half dead by the valiant soldiers of the Pope . . . . . to my mind this wretched prisoner is a thousand times more truly a man than the gloating multitude for whose amusement the Church's spiritual and temporal head and the representative of God on earth is obliged from time to time to provide the spectacle of a severed head.[48]

Notwithstanding the severity of some of his imagined punishments for the misdemeanours of others, Berlioz always felt abhorrence for open cruelty and physical violence. After occasional lone hunting expeditions in his youth and early manhood, this came also to apply to animals, leading him in 1865 to support a protest against the rite of a ceremonial throat-cutting for the shrovetide bull. He congratulates a protester as follows:

No, do not believe you have made yourself look foolish. In any case, to be thought foolish by trivial minds is far better than to be thought callous and insensitive by men of feeling for remaining indifferent to the scenes you so justly stigmatise, which turn so-called civilised man into the nastiest of all predatory animals.[49]

Elsewhere, commenting on the use of falsetto male voices in church, he refers to the "barbarous custom of castration",[50] and in another context to the lack of justice when "a wretched sailor gets fifty lashes for a minor act of insubordination".[51]

Despite the fine overture to which the occasion eventually gave its name, and the corresponding scenes in his opera *Benvenuto Cellini*, that Roman Carnival with the human sacrifice displeased Berlioz in other aspects. The "bloated days, greasy with mire and sweat and grinning painted faces, gross with brutalities and foul-mouthed abuse, drunken informers, whores, half-wits gaping and guffawing, broken-down horses, the reek of the streets, the boredom and degradation of humanity",[52] these things were far from the elevated poetic world of a romantic idealist. Also beyond his ken were the less violent diversions which keep people from serious conversation at social gatherings: he was no gambler or card player, and his utterances on such matters have some ring of a social attitude in addition to indexing his personality. Similarly with birthdays, of which he said to Wagner:

I have a family, I have splendid friends, yet if I had thirty birthdays within the year no one would dream of celebrating even one of them, so well do they know how I dislike all that.[53]

In the same letter he derides his fellow composer for standing on ceremony in modes of address, and on another occasion he feels it necessary to point out — referring to an 1845 portrait of himself by the Viennese artist Prinzhofer — that he has never carried a cane or worn rings, that he is in fact no Dandy; in fairness, though, it must be added that he had his little vanities, such as the famous mop of hair.

If this seems all rather high-minded or falsely modest, it should not be confused with the moralising puritan ethic which he forever detested. A Moscow censor wished to delete some lines from the students' Latin song in *Faust*, as the passage, suggesting that students are wont to search the town at night for girls and sexual conquests, was deemed immoral. Berlioz went through the motions of cutting the offending part from the libretto, though the "prohibited lines were sung at the concert, but in such a way that no one understood them . . . . . I was not going to mutilate my work to satisfy a little vulgar prudery. That would really have been immoral."[54] Philistines must not interefere with his art for prudish reasons; yet, curiously, he could voluntarily relieve a colleague of possible embarrassment arising from similar sexual attitudes. This happened over his delicate choral setting of Victor Hugo's *Sara la Baigneuse*, in which a naked maiden plays and bathes and dreams of being a consort to a rich pasha or sultan. Berlioz told Ferdinand David that "given the great danger there would be in asking the ladies of your singing academy to utter such indecencies, the score is of no use to you".[55]

Here was the tactful man of the world in charge of his emotions, for a while untroubled by provincial attitudes which nevertheless had once deeply wounded him and coloured his whole outlook. When, as a young man, he became finally determined to pursue his musical vocation, he returned to Paris following a total break with his family, his mother saying, after a dreadful confrontation: "You are my son no longer, I curse you!" Berlioz goes on:

> One would hardly believe it possible that even the combination of religious fanaticism with the very grossest contempt for the artistic profession that provincial narrowmindedness is capable of could lead to such a scene . . . . . It was a moment of horror, a scene of grotesque exaggerated violence that I shall never forget, and to it more than to anything I owe my deep hatred of those crass medieval prejudices which still survive in most of the provinces of modern France.[56]

Thus he was pushed towards radical rebellion, tending to turn to Enlightenment thinkers of the previous century for rational guidance, though also inclined to follow those of his contemporaries who attempted to impose a new romantic image of old institutions. Even in strictly musical matters he would quote as authorities names that he happened to admire from other spheres: men such as Cesare Beccaria, an Italian advocate of social and penal reform whose influence spread and persisted long after his death in 1794, and Félicité-Robert de Lamennais, a forceful, music-loving, liberal Catholic. Lamennais, like Chateaubriand and others, acted as herald for a proposed romantic Christian revival to provide the moral basis of a reformed society; but the political aspects of his reformism, at first acceptable to 'ultras' of the Right, eventually became too liberal for comfort in Rome and his ideas were condemned in a Papal Encyclical in 1832. His *Words of a Believer* (1834) presented a rather fundamentalist sort of Christian Socialism based on equality, and by 1848 — when he sat on the extreme Left of the Assembly after the Revolution — he was propounding a religion of Humanity. Commenting on *Words of a Believer* in the course of the letter to Liszt in which he confessed his disbelief in Heaven (page 25) Berlioz said: "Now M. Lamennais has written a sublime book in favour of an idea which seems to me absurd . . . . . is he honest? Equality! Is there such a thing? Is Shakespeare born the equal of M. Scribe? Beethoven the equal of Rossini? "[57]

His early admiration for Lamennais was by now in decline. The romantic who believed in a hierarchy of art and artists, but not in a God who fathered all men, could hardly avoid feeling that some men were fundamentally superior to others. In the matter of musicality he once even went so far as to concede a social class basis for differences, declaring that "nervous sensibility is, in some degree, the heritage of the upper classes of society . . . . . the lower classes, whether it be on account of the manual labour to which they are subject or for any other reason, are comparatively deprived of it".[58] But we move now from social attitudes to the political framework in which Berlioz grew to maturity and must trace his politics from the beginning.

5

How to Change the World

Berlioz's generation was reared during the most expansive and victorious years of Napoleonic grandeur, when France was mistress of Europe and Bonaparte regarded with awe and trembling from the four corners of the earth. They were still children, indeed, when the Congress of Vienna set about restoring some semblance of the old order in 1814-15; but the passions and sufferings of a great epoch were household tales for a decade or more. The oft-betrayed ideals of 1789 lingered still, just beneath the collective consciousness of a France supposed by members of the Holy Alliance to be contented again under a Bourbon monarchy. Some of the Napoleonic mystique was certainly implanted deeply enough in the boy Berlioz to colour his outlook for a lifetime, and while in due course he came to despise both revolutionary republicanism and national patriotism, and fought throughout his life against the narrow attitude to art and thought which sometimes characterised Bonaparte himself, he tended to retain a simple faith in the very name of Napoleon. This was not an uncommon attitude among the Romantics, who often admired the Emperor as a symbol of energy, genius and the triumphant individual, while regretting his tyranny.

Such were the limited political ideas of the young medical student Berlioz when he arrived in Paris in 1821, though he was soon geared to the mood of radical discontent which came to characterise student bodies in restoration Europe. As the 'establishment' of the day was an illiberal Catholic monarchy, his political attitudes moved leftwards — especially after 1824 when the deeply conservative Catholic Charles X mounted the throne. Charles' predecessor Louis XVIII had been to some extent a compromising monarch (after an initial period of extreme reaction to Napoleon's 'hundred days' return in 1815), a balancer of conflicting forces, which had tended to anger the right-wing of royalist-catholic 'ultras'. The new king was more favourable to the latter, and to the Church, and as his reign proceeded the clamps on freedom of expression forced intellectuals into an increasingly anti-clerical position. Extreme Catholic monarchists like Joseph de Maistre and Louis de Bonald remained Bourbon men until their dying day; but while romantic Christians of the Chateau-briand ilk had been inclined originally to welcome a return to the monarchy after 1815, even to the extent of providing literary support for the 'ultras', disillusion followed under Charles X and there was a general move to the left *à la* Lamennais.

The most influential doctrines in this context were those of Saint-Simon, who died in 1825 but left behind a widespread sympathy for his ideas and their offshoots. Comte Claude-Henri de Saint-Simon was a sort of quasi-socialist who has been variously described as a pioneer eager to create a new social system in which all men may develop their faculties through the application of science to industry, and as a medievalist who sought salvation through a revived Christianity. These opposed impressions reflect diverse strands in the outlook of Saint-Simon's eventually fragmented disciples, but undoubtedly many of his schemes were socialistically inclined (while including a paradoxical faith in bankers and industrialists) and envisaged a co-operative technocracy of productive merit working to improve the lot of the under-privileged. His theories were propounded in a naïve conviction that implementation would be quick, easy and bloodless; but while this painless revolution never took place, the 'industrial and scientific' element was perpetuated by an influential group of disciples who studied at the École Poly-technique. Among these were some eventually powerful men who used finance to encourage industrial growth after 1852, during the Second Empire under Louis-Napoleon, who had himself once flirted with Saint-Simonism.

The notion of greater freedom for the expression of ideas and the flowering of creative ability had a natural appeal to socially conscious writers and artists, and for a while the whole Romantic movement in France was influenced by Saint-Simonian doctrines. These dovetailed well with a rebellious outlook inherited from the pre-romantic *Sturm und Drang* period in Germany, which was in some respects the prototype for a Gallic Romanticism partly inspired by the teachings of Mme. de Staël in her influential book *De l'Allemagne*. Growing opposition to the restored *ancien régime* included a substantial element from this wing of radical opinion, typified by the extraordinary gathering of literary and artistic talent, including Berlioz, to support the staging of Victor Hugo's pioneering and overtly romantic poetic drama *Hernani* early in 1830. Such men were allied − not altogether logically in doctrinal terms − with those who wanted more *laissez-faire* economically, a powerful anti-clerical element, and a small but growing working-class eager for a larger slice of the national cake. (Most labouring people were still peasants, but French politics and economics were dominated by the Jacobin inheritance of Paris and Lyons). There were also those who longed for a return to the national glory of the previous decades but who were not to be side-tracked by the minor colonial diversions of Charles X and his ministers.

Feelings on these lines certainly played a part in Berlioz's activities during the 'July Revolution' of 1830. This month was doubly eventful for him, as the revolution started while he was locked in the examination rooms of the 'Institut' making his finally successful attempt (with the *Sardanapale* cantata) to obtain the *Prix de Rome*, giving him a grant for five years, two of which were to be spent in Rome. Already associated with *Les Jeunes-France*, a group of Romantics who later developed republican connections, he left the Institut at the earliest opportunity and sought arms to join the fight for freedom; but the violence had passed its peak and soon the revolution was over. He wrote to his father: "The idea that so many good men have paid with their life for the conquest of our liberties, and that meanwhile I have been useless, upsets me a great deal. It's another anguishing thought added to the rest".[59] Nevertheless he felt inspired, and admired the self-discipline of the people: "The splendid order that reigned during these magical three days is maintained and confirmed; no looting, no lawlessness of any kind. The people have been sublime."[60]

For a change Berlioz felt at one with the people, and stirred by events redolent of Napoleonic triumph he revived Rouget de Lisle's revolutionary song the *Marseillaise* in a version for double chorus and full orchestra. Soon after this he found himself leading a large gathering singing the *Marseillaise* in a Paris arcade, and recalls in his *Memoirs* how at the end of the fourth verse he brought in the crowd of nearly 500 with the refrain — in the spirit of an injunction marked on the score: "everyone with a voice, a soul, and blood in his veins". Thus again Berlioz uses music for a public occasion, a ceremony of shared feelings. This time the subject is not religion but revolutionary patriotism in the manner of his *Hymne à la France* and cantata *The Fifth of May* (originally called *The Death of Napoleon*). Had circumstances been different, Berlioz might during the following few years have produced a great choral symphony commemorating Napoleon's victories, his triumphal return from Italy to Paris, and France's fallen heroes, a scheme he toyed with and then abandoned.

Ten years later a similar ethos (and probably some of the unused Napoleonic music) found expression in the *Funeral and Triumphal Symphony*, an 'open air' work in the ceremonial tradition of Gossec, Méhul and Lesueur, commissioned by the government for a public re-interment of bodies of the heroes whom Berlioz had so admired in 1830. It is doubtful whether by 1840 the patriotic element had much more than token relevance for Berlioz, though when describing composition of the work he wrote with apparent sincerity about the moods to be captured by the various sections. In his notes on the revised finale, a hymn of praise with words by Antony Deschamps which was later extracted for separate use as the *Apothéose*, he describes an ideal performance in which "all eyes were fixed on the high column on which Liberty with wings outspread seemed soaring towards heaven like the souls of those who had given their lives for her".[61] He also went into ecstasies over Victor Hugo's poem *The Return of the Emperor*, published to celebrate the anniversary of Napoleon's death in that same year of 1840 which saw the return of the Emperor's remains from St. Helena to France. But this is Bonaparte again, and by now he had become thoroughly disillusioned with the bourgeois monarchy of Louis-Philippe which had arisen from the 1830 events.

It turned out to be a very modest sort of revolution, replacing oppressive reaction with a cautious, commercially biased conservatism which enthroned a new aristocracy of financiers and industrialists emerging from the middle-classes. There was some enlargement of freedom in expression and criticism, but little alleviation for a still discontented working-class — a process paralleled in Britain by the Reform Bill of 1832, which extended the franchise downwards a little in the cause of economic liberalism rather than democracy. But before this pattern could be foreseen Berlioz reacted with disfavour to the prospect (as it seemed for a time) of a general European upheaval triggered off by the liberal victory in France:

> We are going to have war! Wreckage everywhere. Men who think they are free will hurl themselves against men who are certainly slaves; maybe the free will be exterminated and the slaves will be masters.[62]

He went off to the French Academy in Rome at the start of 1831, as required of Institut prize winners. Here he was already sufficiently detached from the events of the previous July — or sufficiently overwhelmed by the personal problem of his precarious engagement to Camille Moke — to remark that if Papist agitators (who were assailing Frenchmen as revolutionary suspects) had set fire to the Academy, he might have *helped* them! Yet despite the cynicism some revolutionary affinities lingered on. At several points in the *Memoirs* he refers sympathetically to unsuccessful uprisings in Italy and to the Greek revolution, the latter having been the subject of his *Heroic Scene* for chorus and orchestra in 1826. But Greece meant Byron, and the revolts at Modena and Bologna involved members of the Bonaparte family in addition to the radical philosophy of Mazzini, so we may guess that these enthusiasms were as much expressions of romantic hero-worship as of political conviction.

Something which proved to be political by accident was a musical theme chosen to please a Hungarian audience in 1846. This was the famous *Rákóczi March*, used later in *Faust*, his orchestration of which was so successful that the piece became a political weapon for the Hungarians almost overnight, symbolising their dreams of liberty and independence. Although of unknown origins and thus a sort of

folk tune, the march had become associated with Francis II
Rákóczi who led a Hungarian revolt against Austrian rule a
century before Berlioz was born. The authorities in Vienna
were not pleased, and while Berlioz seems to have been una-
ware of the history, his various delighted comments on the
episode show no sympathy for the Austrian Empire. But his
motive in composition was musical nevertheless, drawing on
the emotions of conflict for dramatic purposes — George
Sand remarked that if people revolt, then Berlioz will compose music for the revolution.

But back to Rome in 1831, from whence he wrote just one
year after the July revolution to Charles Duveyrier, editor of
the Saint-Simonist paper *Le Globe*. Berlioz had been discussing politics with the architect Cendrier, a fellow student:

> We have often spoken of you and Saint-Simon. His [Cendrier's]
> cool and calm conviction set me thinking. I read with eagerness a
> file of the *Globe* that someone lent me recently and my last doubts
> have been entirely removed. In whatever concerns the political
> reorganisation of society, I am convinced that Saint-Simon's plan
> is the only true and complete one; [here he states the religious
> reservations mentioned in Chapter 2]. . . . . I suppose this can be no
> bar to my joining my hopes and my energies to yours toward the
> betterment of the larger and poorer class, toward the natural order-
> ing of talents and the destruction of every kind of privilege which,
> hidden like vermin in the folds of the social body, have hitherto
> paralysed all attempts at a remedy.[63]

Here the radical intent is firm and clear, and was indeed regarded as potentially subversive by Prince Metternich, the
Austrian Chancellor, whose censors intercepted the letter.
In economic and political matters this probably represents
the high watermark of Berlioz's leftward feelings, which
thereafter ebbed away rather erratically from the republican/
egalitarian ideal — the Jacobinism whose ghost so troubled
Europe's rulers. In this he contrasts interestingly with the
much admired Hugo, and with the poet Lamartine who, like
Lamennais, started as a royalist but then moved steadily leftwards and eventually became so involved in practical politics
as to be a popular leader in the 1848 revolution — an upheaval
which Berlioz hated.

6

Romantic Disillusion

With the benefit of 20th century hindsight, it might fairly be said that Berlioz's growing disenchantment with politics from 1832 onwards was really an artist's reaction to an increasingly commercial society. He tended to equate a money-grubbing philistine outlook with democracy and republicanism, even though the France of Louis-Philippe was a constitutional monarchy with a very limited franchise, capable of provoking and crushing minor republican revolts of various sorts for a number of years. By modern standards it was not a democracy at all, since the vote was a privilege confined to less than 3% of males over 21: those paying more than a certain annual sum in direct taxes. The latter were mostly on property, not income, so despite two revolutions France was still ruled by landowners — albeit many of them from a new breed of self-made business men. Yet Berlioz, writing to Liszt in 1837, refers to "a régime as weak and unstable as ours . . . . . Oh these representative governments, and cheap ones at that, what a farce! But don't let's talk of that, we won't agree at all, I think. Happily we feel the same about everything else."[64] Liszt, who had joined Berlioz, Saint-Beuve, George Sand and other Romantics in their progressive enthusiasms around 1830, had remained more attached to the teachings of Saint-Simon than his fellow-composer, probably because of the Christian element which Berlioz disdained.

Paradoxically, as early as 1834 the sceptic Berlioz felt able to accept the post of music critic with *Le Rénovateur*, an ultra-royalist-catholic newspaper, saying in excuse (?) to his sister Adèle: "Since I have no use for politics, their shade of opinion does not bother me in the least".[65] However, he was at that time weighed down by financial troubles, being newly married to Harriet Smithson, who brought him debts to settle and was soon to produce a son, so perhaps he may be excused a modest rationalisation — if that is what it was. But very possibly he was by that time already politically neutral in his day-to-day attitudes. Even early in 1832, a mere six months after his bold declaration of Saint-Simonist pro-underdog politics, he responded to a letter from Humbert Ferrand concerning a revolt of weavers at Lyons as follows: ". . . assuredly there is neither absolute good nor absolute evil in politics. Equally certain is it that the heroes of today are the traitors of tomorrow."[66]

In any event, from now on his overriding enthusiasms were musical and his main antipathy the bovine superficiality of the society around him. Comments with political overtones occur from time to time, but usually arise from some frustration seen by Berlioz as imposed by politicians, required by vested interests, or dictated by a philistine ethos. Thus he rails against the "bare-faced appropriations of the poor-house tax-collectors, who take no account of what a concert costs, and contribute to the deficit by walking off with one-eighth of the gross receipts."[67] And elsewhere on the same institution: "Oh, the delights of living in a free country, where artists are serfs, humbly paying their heartfelt tribute to its liberal and equitable laws!"[68]

This is irony with a right-wing flavour, perhaps balanced by his plea for Adolphe Sax who was having great difficulty in the manufacture of new types of musical instrument because of machinations by powerful commercial rivals. Berlioz suggested state-aid in the form of a government order for 300 trumpets and 100 bass tubas, to save Sax and to raise the standard of French military music to that of Prussia and Austria.

Politicians were involved in the stop-go-stop-go farce preceding the *Requiem's* first performance in 1837. Berlioz relates the tale in the *Memoirs*, saying:

> I counsel all struggling artists who read this true account to profit by my experience and ponder what befell me. They will learn the useful if melancholy lesson that in such situations one must trust nobody and nothing, put no more faith in written undertakings than

in spoken ones, and arm oneself against heaven and hell.[69]

There are occasional flashes of his original liberal feelings and sympathy for the economic underdog. In 1851 he visited London as a member of the international jury on musical instruments at the Great Exhibition, and while there he attended a concert given by London's 6500 charity children in St. Paul's Cathedral. Following an ecstatic description of the event, in which he was shattered by a massive rendering of 'All people that on earth do dwell' (but pleased to discover that the music was *not* by Luther, as had once been supposed), he commented on the healthy appearance of the performers, who were "not in the least like the sickly and debilitated young of the working classes in Paris, who are themselves run down by malnutrition, hard work, and privations."[70]

This remark must be seen in the context of an England where various Factory Acts had started to ease the problems of child labour, whereas in France an Act of 1841 which forbade children under eight to work in factories had never been properly enforced. Also, mid-century France was only just entering the phase of massive industrial growth which Britain had pioneered many years before.

On a different note, and in a fantasy in which Berlioz is lightly disguised as Music petitioning a Minister in a democratic republic, he says:

> At the coming of liberty, equality and fraternity, I believed for a moment in my coming liberation; but I was mistaken. When the hour of Negro emancipation struck, I indulged in fresh hopes; I was again mistaken.[71]

His mistake, as he saw it, was to believe that republics would be any more tolerant of the arts than monarchies; or to have faith in the noble people, which turned out to be an ignoble mob. Such a mob moved him to bitter words during the European upheavals of 1848, when Prince Felix Lichnowsky, active on the Right in the short-lived German National Assembly, was tortured and left to die by a Frankfurt crowd during nationalist riots against the Malmoe Truce, a Prussian inspired ceasefire between Denmark and the German States following a dispute about Schleswig-Holstein. "Vile human scum, a thousand times more bestial and brainless in your fatuous revolutionary antics than the baboons and orang-outangs of

Borneo!"[72] But anger with left-wing revolutionaries did not make him a proponent of capitalism; indeed he attacked capitalists in the unlikely context of his *Treatise on Modern Instrumentation and Orchestration*, pointing out that they would spend thousands on investments but would not even spare a thought to honour the great art of music.

At heart, Berlioz was a humane aristocrat who would have liked democracy to work but who found its limited application in the bourgeois society of his own time inimicable to his art. Political upheavals, revolutions, *coups d'état* — all tended to worsen the lot of the artist, and while always wishing to maximise freedom, he longed above all for peaceable order in a climate of respect for culture. This he tended to find outside France, particularly in Germany and Russia where he discovered despotic but cultivated and benevolent rulers who honoured music without assuming that it should make a profit.

Because of dictatorial efficiency his music did indeed sometimes make substantial profits in princedoms and absolute monarchies. Writing to Ferrand in 1841, Berlioz mentions a successful performance of the *Requiem* in St. Petersburg "by the combined forces of all the opera houses, the Czar's chapel, and the choruses of the two regiments of the Imperial Guard. Thanks to the munificence of the Russian nobility, the admirable Romberg, who conducted, made a profit of five thousand francs. When it comes to art, give me a despotic government! In Paris, to put on the whole work, I would have to be mad or prepared to lose what Romberg made."[73]

This sort of experience was paralleled on his German tours, perhaps explaining the fact that his imaginary future city of Euphonia is situated within the German empire and is very far from democratic in its organisation. He actually advocated dictatorship in the theatre:

> Despotism is necessary: supremely intelligent in kind no doubt; but after all — despotism. It must be military despotism; the despotism of a commander-in-chief; or of an admiral, in time of war. Outside these or similar conditions, there can be nothing but incomplete results, counter-sense, disorder and cacophany.[74]

Berlioz had successes in England comparable with those achieved in Germany, but somehow never came to admire

that country as much as the minor kingdoms in central
Europe. Perhaps the metropolis of the most advanced industrial nation was too massive and impersonal for this most
personal of artists (it was already by far the world's largest
city) and there were certainly many parallels between English
and French bourgeois attitudes which he would have found
distasteful.

He happened to be in London during the 1848 upheavals
in Paris, which he observed with disapproval. After an initial
spasm of national euphoria following the February revolution, France descended rapidly into chaos to become what
Berlioz called a "republic of pickpockets and costermong-
ers."[75] The new regime was at first ideologically well to the
Left, but universal male suffrage in a predominantly peasant
society produced a shift to the Right in the National Assembly
and the government became steadily less radical. The resent-
ments and insecurities which had grown and festered during
Louis-Philippe's reign then exploded: a frustrated Paris
working-class resorted to violence and the bourgeoisie responded with gruesome counterviolence in the famous 'June days'.
Aggravated by a general European slump which reached its na-
dir not long before the uprising, the viciously class-conscious
turn of events seemed for a while to fit the philosophy of the
recently published *Communist Manifesto*, although Marx
himself scoffed at the idea of effective revolution in a still
largely agricultural France. The immediate disruption was
eased when Louis-Napoleon was chosen as President at the
end of 1848; but three more years of uncertainty were to
elapse — with revolt, election, counter-election, expansion
and contraction of the franchise, repression, and much political bargaining — before this latter-day Bonaparte seized
power beyond the Presidency, prior to establishing the Second
Empire as Napoleon III in 1851/1852.

Berlioz, it seems, saw right through all the humbug and
expected (wished for!) some sort of dictatorship in due
course once Louis-Napoleon was elected in 1848: ". . . . . the
peasants . . . . . base great expectations on the good advice
the emperor [Napoleon I] will give his nephew, for they
know exactly what value to attach to the lie about the
emperor's death".[76] Victor Hugo, who unlike Berlioz had
become steadily *more* radical and politically active, joined
many other liberals in supporting the President's election

but was outraged when he abandoned the short-lived Second Republic to become an Emperor (shades of Beethoven's disillusion with Napoleon I fifty years before!). He then went into exile and conducted a fierce campaign against Napoleon III from the Channel Isles, but Berlioz only poked fun:

> Hugo, furious at not being made Emperor!* . . . . . I am an out-and-out imperialist; I shall never forget that our Emperor rescued us from the vile stupid republic! All civilised beings should remember that. He has the misfortune to be a barbarian in art matters; but what of that! He is a barbarian who has saved society — after all, Nero was an artist . . . . .[77]

For once Berlioz puts society above art; but in *Evenings with the Orchestra* (10th Evening) another side of him responded to the events of 1848 by comparing musical and social matters on an equal footing. He equated the manner in which the Paris authorities decreed a musical education for working-class children (only to frustrate it by means of rigid educational techniques) with the politician Louis Blanc's socialistically inclined National Workshops, which at one point involved creating employment by digging holes and then refilling them. It was the projected closure of the latter which had sparked off the worst violence in Paris. The Romantic in him applauded free musical education (shades of Euphonia), and a remaining radical streak wanted to reduce poverty by means of full employment (shades of Saint-Simon), but his rationalism could not abide the senseless mis-application of either (shades of Voltaire). Also in 1848, writing from London to the architect Joseph-Louis Duc, he shows a nicely balanced detachment on political matters when explaining that the dedication of his *Apothéose* to Duc could not be printed on the English edition because this would have drawn attention to the Bastille Column in Paris, a monument conceived by Duc to commemorate those who fell in the 1830 revolution:

> . . . . . since the last Chartists' agitation the London bourgeois has a deep fear of anything remotely or nearly related to revolutions, and as a result my publisher refused to consider any mention on the title page either of your monument or of those to whom it was put up.[78]

But the detachment fled later in the same letter when he came

*Hugo had expected to become a member of the government after Louis-Napoleon's election.

to deal with friends who had reproached him for not returning to Paris during the third French Revolution:

> A man must have a tricolour flag over his eyes not to be able to see
> that music in France is dead and that it is the last of the arts our
> rulers are going to take any notice of. They tell me I'm holding aloof
> from my country. I don't hold aloof from it: I flee from it as one
> flees from a barbaric shore when one is looking for civilisation,
> and I have done so not only since the Revolution. For long now I
> have stifled my love of France and uprooted from my heart the
> foolish habit of centring all my thoughts on her.

This 'foolish habit' of self-centred nationalism, particularly
any variety involving revolutionary upheavals, was one of
Berlioz's steady anathemas from the mid 1830s onwards. In
another letter written from London in 1848, in which he
described the Chartists' demonstration of April that year, he
expressed relief that the event passed off peacefully in face
of overwhelming might in the form of assembled cannons:

> They [the cannons] were not even obliged to speak, the sight of
> them was enough to drive into the heads of all the conviction that a
> revolution was ill-timed, and the Chartists dispersed in good order.
> Worthy fellows! You know nearly as much about insurrections as
> the Italians do about writing symphonies. It's the same probably
> with the Irish, and O'Connell was right in always saying: 'Agitate,
> agitate! But do not budge!'[79]

Nicely ambiguous, this last remark. Was he poking fun at
politicians who call for action but will not take it, or adopting an air of wisdom in the tradition of Edmund Burke by
asserting that social change must be gradual? However, an
awareness of Daniel O'Connell and his careful fight for
oppressed Catholic Ireland is understandable, as O'Connell
had been represented in France for many years as a supreme
Celtic hero; Balzac even equated him with Napoleon when
listing the great men of the century. But this is part of a
curious tangle of attitudes to be examined in the next chapter.

Returning to Berlioz's views on nationalism in general: to
the modern mind there is some contradiction between devotion to a series of small monarchies on the one hand and an
overriding internationalism on the other, though from the
artist's viewpoint it is not necessarily illogical. He appreciated

personal aristocratic patronage from one and saw that ordered, peaceful existence was threatened if patriotic passions
were not subdued by the other.

Commenting on the 1845 celebrations in Bonn, when a
statue was erected to honour Beethoven, Berlioz criticised
the organisers for not employing Europe's best musicians
in the official orchestra. All that was needed "was to apply
six months in advance, to the leading instrumentalists . . . . .
and keep clear of any narrow ideas of nationalism . . . . . they
can only have disastrous results and are bound to appear
infinitely ridiculous to all right-minded people!'[80] Ironically,
this was in the Germany that he loved, and where he was to
meet some difficulty with his setting of *Faust*, both because
he was a Frenchman who had dared to tamper with Goethe's
masterpiece, and because he had the audacity to locate his
hero in Hungary instead of the Fatherland. His response?
To declare that patriotism was a fetish of cretins and to
remark that "for sheer ludicrous ferocity there is nothing to
compare with a fanatical German nationalist fully roused."[81]

On another occasion he had included in a concert programme a chorus from Halévy's *Charles VI* which happened
to have some anti-English lines. This was at a time when
Louis-Philippe was endeavouring to improve Anglo-French
relations in the face of jingoistic opposition. The audience
joined in with the chorus and Berlioz was summoned to
police headquarters on the suspicion that he had been politically motivated in playing Halévy's piece. Berlioz refers to
the audience's reaction as "a crudely nationalistic protest"
and declared to the Commissioner of Police that he "could
not be less sympathetic to the kind of nationalistic frenzy
which can get inflamed in 1844 over an incident from the
reign of Charles VI".[82] *

Nationalist inflammation of a protectionist kind was in
the air sixteen years later in response to the Anglo-French
Treaty of Commerce, which established a substantial degree
of free-trade between the two countries. Propounded by
Richard Cobden for England, this agreement was applied in
France during one of Napoleon III's more liberal phases by
Michael Chevalier, a neo-Saint-Simonist whose ideal was
prosperity through co-operative economic expansion. The

*Charles VI reigned 1380-1422.

Treaty was followed by various expressions of cross-channel devotion during 1860, and Berlioz was involved in producing a work for massive double chorus to be sung in both languages at the Crystal Palace in 1861. But the dual performance never took place and *Le Temple Universel* was eventually re-written for a single chorus. It is not known whether the words (by Vaudin) were specially commissioned by Berlioz, but they certainly include an element of Saint-Simonian internationalism that could have appealed to the anti-jingoist in him:

> No more barriers
> For the children of labour and art!
> Let us embrace across our frontiers,
> Europe shall one day fly a single flag.

But if this small outburst of brotherly love was a musical opportunity grasped for convenience rather than an ideological assertion made from conviction, there is strong evidence that Berlioz's internationalism was not always a mere neo-musical phenomenon. For instance, he wrote with strong feeling to the Princess Sayn-Wittgenstein in 1866 when the Austro-Prussian war was raging. This conflict brought together Berlioz's abhorrence of violence, his contempt for unthinking national devotion, and his general feelings about the military and political men who make history:

> As for famous men who were not artists, I am beginning to be tired of them. Those poor little scoundrels who are called great men fill me with nothing but overwhelming horror. Caesar, Augustus, Antony, Alexander, Philip, Peter and so many others, were no better than bandits .... And the war! Oh yes, this is the right moment to speak of that. To speak of the hundreds of thousands of idiots who are cutting one another's throats, slitting one another's bellies, shooting one another at close range and dying furiously in mud and blood, in obedience to three or four rascals who take care to do no fighting themselves, and with no clear understanding of the pretexts invoked to lead them to this butchery![83]

Thus the humanitarian Berlioz, who three years before writing this letter had made a speech at Strasbourg following a concert given as part of a Rhineland Festival:

> You have rightly said, Sir, that under the influence of music the soul is uplifted, the mind broadens, civilisation progresses, and

national hatreds dwindle. See how France and Germany mingle on this day: the love of art brings them together and this worthy love will do more for their complete union than the wonderful Rhine bridge and other modes of rapid transport in use between the two countries.[84]

Alas, in a century since his death neither art nor transport have conquered the world's divisions. Perhaps it is well that he died before the Franco-Prussian bloodbath of 1870 and the subsequent compulsive pattern of violent revolt and repression in the Paris Commune, which would surely have broken an already disillusioned heart.

7

A Celtic Backcloth

The subject of this chapter is a curiosity, something that refuses to fit conveniently into a scheme of ideology and intellect yet which cannot be dismissed as a mere biographical detail. In one sense it is political and literary, for it involves a musical juxtaposition of politics and poetry, but in a manner deeply entwined with Berlioz's personal attitudes. It starts with 'Élégie', a song based on words of Thomas Moore and written for tenor solo with piano accompaniment. This was first published in 1830 as the final item in *Neuf Mélodies*, a group of songs later renamed *Irlande* in deference to Moore's *Irish Melodies* which provided the texts.

This Irish poet's verse is for the most part very direct, and, excepting its frequent historical allusions, may be absorbed without much need to ponder over hidden depths of meaning. Yet though Moore lacks the multi-layered metaphor of Shakespeare, Berlioz seemed at times to place him next to the Bard in his private poetic pantheon. For instance, in the monodrama *Lélio*, sequel to the *Fantastic Symphony* in which the artist emerges from his opium dream, Berlioz declares that "Shakespeare has wrought a change in me, has revolutionized my inmost being. Moore, with his dolorous melodies, has completed thy work, thou creator of Hamlet".

Berlioz relates in his *Memoirs* how, in a dazed state brought about by the impact of *Hamlet* and the histrionic powers of Harriet Smithson as Ophelia at the Odéon Theatre in 1827, he "wandered aimlessly about the Paris streets and the neighbouring plains. During that long period of affliction I recall only four occasions when I really slept." One of these sleeps was in the snow by the banks of the frozen Seine, so his distraction must have lasted for several months after Harriet's September performances. He goes on:

> It was on my return from one of these wanderings (during which I looked like a man searching for his soul) that I came upon my copy of Moore's *Irish Melodies* lying open on the table at the poem which begins 'When he who adores thee' and, taking up my pen, wrote the music to that heartrending farewell straight off . . . . This is the sole occasion on which I was able to express a feeling of the sort directly in music while still under its active influence. But I think I have rarely found a melody of such truth and poignancy, steeped in such a surge of sombre harmony . . . . To catch its true meaning — that is to recreate more or less faithfully the mood of pride and tenderness and deep despair which Moore must have experienced when he wrote the words, and which I felt when my music flooded out and took possession of them — two accomplished artists are needed . . . . To hear it poorly done would be inexpressibly painful for me. That is why, in all the twenty years of its existence, I have never asked anyone to sing it to me.[85]

Berlioz retained very deep feelings about 'Élégie', and could hardly bear even to imagine it being performed by fallible mortals. He left it intact and seemed to regard it as untouchable despite the fact that it is in a genre quite uncharacteristic of the mature composer. He once made a start on orchestrating the piano accompaniment following a spontaneous and moving rendering by the singer Louis Alizard, but he then "reflected that works of this kind are not meant for the ordinary concert-going public; to expose them to its indifference would be a kind of sacrilege, and I broke off and destroyed as much as I had done".[86] The words, an 1823 French prose version of Moore's lines, were also left alone. Consequently, apart from short linking passages in the operas, 'Élégie', is the only piece of secular music in Berlioz's whole output to use a non-poetic text. It thus stands apart from other songs in *Irlande* in not drawing upon the talents of Thomas Gounet, whose verse translations Berlioz employed when tackling the cycle as a whole in 1829. Here is Thomas Moore's original poem, which Berlioz was later pleased to discover fitted his music almost as well as the prose that inspired his composition in 1827:

WHEN HE WHO ADORES THEE

When he who adores thee has left but the name
  Of his fault and his sorrows behind,
Oh! say, wilt thou weep, when they darken the fame
  Of a life that for thee was resign'd?
Yes, weep, and however my foes may condemn,
  Thy tears shall efface their decree;
For Heaven can witness, though guilty to them,
  I have been but too faithful to thee.

With thee were the dreams of my earliest love,
  Every thought of my reason was thine;
In my last humble prayer to the Spirit above,
  Thy name shall be mingled with mine.
Oh! blest are the lovers and friends who shall live
  The days of thy glory to see;
But the next dearest blessing that Heaven can give
  Is the pride of thus dying for thee.

Berlioz's setting of this achieves a passionate intensity practically unique in French song, and it would be a reasonable
conjecture that he placed his first-born 'Irish Melody' at the
end of the complete cycle because he felt that its elevated
mood could not be equalled and should not be shattered. It
was a sort of Amen. Yet Moore's lines are not especially
striking, certainly not in French prose or for anyone with
Shakespeare ringing in his ears. Ostensibly the poet seems to
be a spirit bidding adieu to his loved-one after a sacrificial
death; but although the unobtainable and Irish-accented Miss
Smithson had clearly overwhelmed the infatuated Berlioz, it
seems rash to attribute his unique reaction to Moore's words
solely to the slight coincidence of his own unrequited love
and the lost love suggested by the poem. Incidentally, it
should be mentioned that Berlioz's claim that 'Élégie', was
composed in 1827 cannot be validated. He actually referred
to a recent violently disturbing episode of work on the song
in a letter written early in 1830, although this may have been
when he was adding the piano accompaniment to his original
vocal melody. In any event, the Smithson/Élégie connection
obviously became very firm in his mind and he certainly read
the Moore translations at the earlier date, for he sent a copy
to his sister in January 1828 with an enthusiastic recom-
mendation.

Whether in 1827 or 1830, Moore's lines clearly made a tremendous impression. Perhaps Berlioz sensed the poem's real import at some unconscious level, where it continued to trouble him. When he discovered in London over twenty years later that Moore had intended the person speaking in the verses to be the Irish revolutionary patriot Robert Emmet, who died on the gallows in 1803, Berlioz did not simply dismiss the matter as a problem solved, but felt sufficiently committed even then to write an explanatory note to go with his 'Élégie'. This preface, which he still thought worth publishing as late as 1863 (Richault edition of *33 Mélodies*), relates some of the tragic story, including a reference to Emmet's love for a girl called Sarah Curran. Berlioz seems to have remained confused about who Moore intended Emmet's loved-one to be in the poem, being inclined to think that it must be Sarah. However, it is clear now that it was really the patriot's native land Ireland, an idealistic devotion to which Moore had shared with Emmet when they were fellow students in Dublin in 1795-98.

Berlioz ended his note on the verses by expressing puzzlement about the 'fault' confessed in the poem's second line — for he could not know that this was the one true reference to Sarah, some letters from whom had been discovered when Emmet was arrested and about which he felt acutely guilty, as they should have been destroyed. But whether or not the composer appreciated what Moore had in mind regarding the details, his feelings on the story as a whole were such that he included with his preface some passages from the speech made by Emmet to his judge during the trial. Some of Berlioz's excerpts are given below — a tiny part only of the full speech, which is a minor classic in the literature of freedom, admired among others by the young Abraham Lincoln:

> Where is the boasted freedom of your constitution?
> Where the impartiality, mildness and clemency of your court of justice, if a wretched culprit about to be delivered over to the executioner be not suffered to vindicate his motives? . . . . As a man to whom fame is dearer than life, I will use the last moments of that life in rescuing my name and memory from the foul and odious imputations thrown upon them. . . . . . My lord, I have been sacrificed on the altar of truth and liberty. There have I extinguished the torch of friendship and offered up the idol of my soul, the

object of my affections. There have I parted with all that could be dear to me in this life, and nothing now remains to me but the cold honours of the grave. My lamp of life is nearly extinguished. . . . . All that I request at my departure from this world is the charity of its silence. Let no man write my epitaph. And as no man who knows my motives dares to vindicate them, so let no man who is ignorant of them with prejudice asperse them, till my country has taken her rank amongst the nations of the earth. Then only can my epitaph be written, and then alone can my character be vindicated.

Although in 1827 Berlioz's sympathies would probably have been with the rebellious Irishman (if he had known the real subject of Moore's poem), by the time he learnt about Emmet in 1851 he had become thoroughly disillusioned with radical/ nationalist politics. Yet he still felt impelled to quote Emmet's speech with fervent approval, obliging his publisher to print the original English as well as a French version of Emmet's words. Why? Was it lip-service paid to the happy spirit of revolt remembered from 1830? Or perhaps a feeling of obliga- tion to Moore for following an honoured poetic tradition in commemorating a radical martyr? Wordworth had done the latter in his sonnet to the great negro leader Toussaint l'Ouverture of San Domingo (Haiti), who languished in a Paris prison for opposing Napoleon's edict re-establishing slavery — such was the French quest for Liberty by 1802. Ironically, he died in the same year as Emmet, who had hoped for a while to enlist that very Napoleon in the fight for Irish freedom. But great art survives the occasions which give it birth: however overwhelming the struggle and the agony of the moment, a hero's ideals last longer in a poem than in the flux of politics. Few have heard of Toussaint today, but we may still be stirred by the closing lines of Wordsworth's tribute:

> There's not a breathing of the common wind
> That will forget thee; thou hast great allies;
> Thy friends are exultations, agonies,
> And love, and man's unconquerable mind.

In just such a commemorative mood, Berlioz and other French Romantics had echoed Chateaubriand in apotheosizing the poet André Chénier, who died in 1794 under the Terror of Robespierre. Despite its origin as a 'March of the Guards' in the abandoned opera *Les Francs-Juges*, the 'March to the Scaffold' from the *Fantastic Symphony* is probably an echo of the Chénier story, a tale of creative youth cut short by fanatical violence which has inspired a number of musicians, notably Giordano in his opera *Andrea Chénier*.

But youth cut short in the figure of Robert Emmet was in Berlioz's case part of an obsession with things Irish which seems to have been more fundamental to his soul than an instinct for radical protest. Time and again he refers to Moore's *Irish Melodies* as a source of deeply felt poetic emotion, a group of feelings often presented by the poet as a Celtic dream of love, heroism and natural art set in a gentle, antique landscape: in part a recital of images for defining one aspect of Romanticism. Another aspect is evoked by Sir Walter Scott's words chosen by Berlioz to head the score of his *Waverley* overture:

> Dreams of love and Lady's charms
> Give place to honour and to arms.

Scott's first novel was hardly as chivalrous and medieval as this would suggest (it was actually set in the 18th century), but the tone was historical/romantic and thus appropriate to the age and to the young Berlioz, who composed both the *Waverley* and *Francs Juges* overtures in 1827, the year in which he discovered Moore, Shakespeare and Harriet Smithson. Conceived originally as an opera, *Les Francs Juges* concerns a darkly sinister aspect of medieval Germany, where private courts inflicted horrible punishments. Berlioz was repelled by the horror but felt impelled to capture its mood in music. In this he echoed his time, as fascination with a mysterious and sometimes terrifying past had crept over literary Europe.

Before the French Revolution, a public ready for its first trips into a romantic dream-world had eagerly followed a series of epic tales translated from the Gaelic of the ancient bard Ossian by James Macpherson. Goethe and Beethoven were among Ossian's many eminent admirers, and although Macpherson was eventually shown to be more of a fabricator than a translator, the appetite for Celtic poetry had been whetted throughout the Continent. This was eventually paralleled by a revival of interest in folk culture generally, sometimes as part of an emerging nationalism as happened

in Germany with Arnim's and Brentano's collection entitled
Youth's Magic Horn, which followed the pioneering research-
es of Herder and inspired the Grimm brothers' Fairy Tales.
Anything of beauty whose origins were untainted by the
ordered elegance of 18th century forms became popular, particularly old ballads of the type popularised by Thomas
Percy's *Reliques of Ancient English Poetry*, or the traditional
sagas to be found at the extremities of Europe's 'offshore
islands'. A passion for the latter was epitomised on a grand
scale by the Scotsman George Thomson, who collected great
quantities of melodies and verses from Scotland, Wales and
Ireland and commissioned various poets (including Burns and
Scott) to improve or replace the words, and a number of
famous composers (such as Haydn and Beethoven) to arrange
the tunes. Thomson's activities in Edinburgh were soon
emulated by the Power brothers in Dublin, who employed
Thomas Moore to write verses for various collections of Irish
melodies based on ancient airs. For many of these old tunes
Moore drew upon the folksong collections of his contemporary Edward Bunting, but he also adapted the melodies as
necessary — being a moderately accomplished musician —
before passing them on to John Stevenson who did the har-
monies and accompaniments for the publishers. The resulting
ballads became enormously popular in Britain, and some of
the verses — together with Moore's long poem *The Loves of
the Angels* — found their way into a French prose translation:
the volume in which Berlioz later discovered the poet's veiled
tribute to Robert Emmet.*

Several of the songs have remained popular for 150 years
and are now firmly embedded in Anglo-Saxon (not to say
Celtic) folklore: who has not heard of *The Minstrel Boy* or
the *Last Rose of Summer*? Beethoven made arrangements of
both, while the 'Last Rose' was also the subject of a piano
Fantasy by Mendelssohn and appeared as an aria in Flotow's
opera *Martha* — a dull work which Berlioz thought was saved
only by the interpolated Irish air, as "its perfume is almost
enough to disinfect the rest of the score".[87] Schumann
derived his *Paradise and the Peri* from Moore's long oriental
fantasy *Lalla Rookh*, which was the basis of no less than

---

*Les amours des anges et les mélodies irlandaises de Thomas Moore translated by
Louise S. Belloc (Paris 1823).

seven operas, and parts of which joined other Moore poems in inspiring a host of minor composers in a variety of vocal pieces.

Friend of Shelley and Byron (of whom Moore became the official biographer), the Irish poet managed to underplay his early radicalism without actually denying it, and was for long stretches the idol of London society. Byron, incidentally, happened to be particularly fond of Moore's own musical setting of 'When he who adores thee', while the Irishman's poetry as a whole generated an idealistic haze of bitter-sweet nostalgia which appealed equally to struggling Irish patriots or comfortable English aristocrats. It also resonated perfectly with the strain of pseudo-Celtic Romanticism which had started with Macpherson's Ossian and now flourished in post-Napoleonic Europe.

In France especially, from the Restoration until about the middle of the century, the Romantics admired all things Irish. Many comments on Erin, its people and its problems appeared in Paris newspapers during the 1820s and 30s, especially in *Le Globe*; writers like Thomas Moore and Lady Morgan (a sort of self-appointed Irish Muse) were quickly translated and eagerly read; Irish performers on the stage (Harriet Smithson) or in the concert hall (John Field) were praised ecstatically; Stendhal attempted an analysis of Irish culture in terms of the special sensationalist psychology he had elaborated from the Idéologue philosophers; the great radical/romantic historian Jules Michelet went on a fact-finding tour of Ireland; and so on.

One small item in this ferment of Irish interest appeared as a sentimentally exaggerated article about Robert Emmet and Sarah Curran in the *Revue de Paris* of January 1831, and it is interesting to speculate whether, if Berlioz had read this, he would have connected the story with 'When he who adores thee'. But he was on the first stage of his journey to Italy when the article appeared, and probably missed it. A little later, in Rome, he composed his *Religious Meditation* using a Moore text and pieced together the scenario of *Lélio*, which was partly modelled on the Irishman's *Melologue Upon National Airs* and included the glowing reference to Moore mentioned earlier. It was in some respects symptomatic of the Irish cult in France that a young man could go from Paris to Italy and remain concerned with nostalgic Celtic poetry in the midst of sun-baked classical ruins.

But this cultural setting notwithstanding, and even allowing that Berlioz's eventual marriage to Harriet may have
strengthened any feelings of Irish allegiance, it remains a
striking oddity of his character that he could be stirred so
very easily and powerfully by anything to do with Ireland.
For instance, the modest songs of his Irish pianist/composer
friend George Osborne led him to declare:

> Nothing stimulates my imagination more than those pure, fresh
> melodies, so original yet so natural, which take one straight to the
> green hills of Ireland and seem to come carried on the evening
> breeze softly across the rippling lakes of Killarney — those odes to
> long-suffering love which move one without one's knowing why,
> and turn one's thoughts to solitude and the grandeur of nature,
> loved ones who are no more, heroes of old, a country's woes, and
> death itself.[88]

The casually familiar references here to green hills and to the
evening breeze over the lakes of Killarney are remarkable for
a man who never crossed the Irish Sea. Also, 'a country's
woes and death itself' suggest the Emmet syndrome again,
while the passage as a whole conveys something of the
involuntary flood of feeling which possessed the composer
in 1827 when he first responded to Moore's thoughts with a
flash of white-hot musical creativity. Berlioz's belief that
Moore had penned those thoughts in a 'mood of pride and
tenderness and deep despair' is also very curious, since he
expressed this view *before* he learnt about Emmet and despite
a footnote printed beneath the original translation stating
that the poem was based on an ancient Irish story. How
could he have known that Moore's personal feelings were so
deeply involved?

Such oddities, coupled with Berlioz's compulsive need —
after twenty-four years — to ferret out the occasion for the
lines from Moore's friend Leigh Hunt when he was in London,
have prompted a closer look at Robert Emmet. The author
felt that there may be other links between the French composer and the Irish revolutionary to explain why, when one
of them accidentally stumbled upon a disguised tribute to the
other, he reacted with an intense emotion strong enough to
leave its imprint for a life-time. The enquiry has revealed a
number of coincidences which prompt speculations extending

beyond this book's central plan, which is to examine the composer's conscious beliefs, feelings and interests. Unconscious influences, perhaps even some occult ones, seem to surround the Emmet connection. Prudence therefore suggests that this psychic byway be relegated to an appendix, to which believers and sceptics alike may react as they wish after following the more conventional Berlioz through to Chapter 13.

But of course the 'conventional' Berlioz was still exceptionally volatile, motivated obscurely by extremes of feeling extending beyond normal bounds. Thus he would respond urgently to certain types of impulse, and it could be that the particular set of ideas expressed in Moore's poem just happened to provide the one ideal key needed for an instant musical reaction — a response in such perfect resonance with the poetry and with his own temperament that Berlioz unthinkingly projected his feelings onto the poet when he wrote about the 'pride, tenderness and despair' he had felt in 1827. Curiously, in his 'Essay on the Music of Ireland' (normally printed as a preface to *Irish Melodies*) Thomas Moore himself noted just such a match between the music and temper of the Irish people:

> The tone of defiance, succeeded by the languor of despondency — a burst of turbulence dying away into softness — the sorrows of one moment lost in the levity of the next — and all that romantic mixture of mirth and sadness, which is naturally produced by the efforts of a lively temperament to shake off or forget the wrongs which lie upon it. Such are the features of our history and character, which we find strongly and faithfully reflected in our music.

This could easily have been Berlioz describing himself, and it would certainly serve as an impression of much of his music, perhaps signifying a natural affinity of moods and attitudes to draw him towards all things Irish. However, his music had its own special ways of evoking languor or levity, turbulence or sorrow, ways concerned very much with the blending or contrasting of instrumental sound qualities. In such matters he had a special passion and expertise.

8

Sounds of the Spirit

Berlioz had an abnormal sensitivity to sound qualities as an integral part of music, as a basic dimension to parallel pitch, rhythm and dynamics. Today, his use of instrumental tone-colour as a structural element in expanding the expressive boundaries of music is legendary; but as the subject loomed so large in his thoughts and played an important part in his campaigns for artistic expressiveness, and as it can be discussed without recourse to musical theory, it has this chapter to itself.

Berlioz not only regarded himself as a torchbearer leading on from Beethoven in the belief that music can play some unique part in the spiritual life of man, but also expanded and enriched the sonic materials available to all composers. In an age when the orchestra was itself becoming a large and flexible instrument rather than a mere collection of instrumentalists, he charted the way with his own magnificent scoring. He also preached what he practised, in articles, in a massive correspondence, and in his *Treatise on Modern Instrumentation and Orchestration*, first published in 1844 and still a standard work on the subject, two lifetimes later. He was also the first to produce a manual on the art of conducting (*Chef d'Orchestre*), added to the *Treatise* in 1855. There are few composers since that time who have not referred to the work on occasion. Some have even taught themselves from it. Though nominally a technical thesis, the *Treatise* makes very lively reading even for those who cannot follow a score. A later edition was revised and annotated by that great orchestrator Richard Strauss, who acknowledged his huge debt to Berlioz near the end of his life.

Although Berlioz always showed a keen interest in new musical instruments — hence his championship of Adolphe Sax and his choice as a judge at the 1851 Exhibition — the 'new' sounds employed in his own music arose almost without exception from careful use of established or recently perfected instruments. His book shows extraordinary insight regarding playing techniques, quite apart from the ways in which various sound qualities can or should be used in orchestration. Whether it be the use of additional fingers to produce difficult pizzicato effects on the violin; or the misuse of pedals by pianists who rate their personal vanity above a composer's intentions; or the need for more drums and drummers to minimise retuning activities during orchestral works; or the compilation of a chart to reveal the changes of timbre and facility of execution, on the violin, of all the major and minor keys, arising from the numbers of open strings employed; or the advocacy of a wayward use of the string bass to achieve 'a loud female cry' by pinching the high string near to the bridge; all these and many other points are covered in the *Treatise*, and then only in passing as a mere prelude to the actual task of balancing sound qualities against each other.

More than any previous composer, Berlioz used instrumental tone-colour as part of his musical structure rather than simply to enhance a drama inherent in the musical ideas before orchestration. This expanded the dramatic and expressive functions of music itself, often in a manner unacceptable to his contemporaries. Thus his use of a pair of anguished sliding notes on a double-bass to portray Cleopatra's actual dying gasp in the cantata *Death of Cleopatra*, rather than a few conventional minor chords to round things off after her last words, was regarded as altogether too weird by the judges who rejected this work at his third attempt to gain the Prix de Rome in 1829. Such convention-bound responses helped to make him into a campaigner for instrumental expressiveness, with the *Treatise* as a sort of campaign guide. It is packed with ideas, both in abstraction and by examples from his own and other composers' work. Here are eleven points culled at random, covering cor anglais, cellos and basses, piano, violins, harp, harp with woodwind, mandolin, clarinet, trombones with flutes, timpani and bass drum.[89]

In the pastoral movement of the *Fantastic Symphony* (a

work composed only three years after the death of Beethoven, and — with *Harold in Italy*, *Romeo and Juliet* and the
Requiem — written before Wagner had started any of his
major projects) Berlioz uses the cor anglais to repeat frag-
ments of an earlier exchange of phrases with an oboe, this
reiteration being to the accompaniment of four timpani, with
the rest of the orchestra silent. The composer claims — and
we can only agree — that "the feelings of absence, of forget-
fulness, of sorrowful loneliness, which arise . . . on hearing
this forsaken melody would lack half their power if played
by an instrument other than the cor anglais". Unselfishly, he
also acknowledges and commends Meyerbeer as the first to
mix the low sounds of the cor anglais with the bass notes of
horns and clarinets during a double-bass tremolo, to give "a
sonority as peculiar as it is novel, and well suited to colour,
with its menacing impression, ideas in which fear and solici-
tude predominate". The relatively dark, 'romantic' character
associated with the cor anglais in comparison with the other
woodwinds is paralleled by the viola when set against the
violins. Hence Berlioz's use of this instrument to represent
the melancholy, brooding character of Childe Harold in
Harold in Italy — another example of mood painting by
means of tone-colour.

On the use of cellos and string basses, Berlioz warns that
composers should not entirely separate their parts without
'excellent reason', but then gives an example of fully justified
separation from his *Requiem*, where in one passage the cellos
go an octave all but a minor-second *beneath* the basses in
order to combine a discordant musical effect with the sonic
effect of open cello strings against stopped double-bass strings.

The piano is not readily associated with Berlioz, yet he
knew sufficient of its qualities to employ it, played by four
hands, for a unique quivering effect to accompany a chorus
of airy spirits in the *Tempest Fantasia* (now normally part
of *Lélio*). He used the instrument in this special manner not
just to be different, but to produce an otherwise unobtainable effect. Musical expressiveness was his object, which is
why this reputedly noisy, vulgar, brassy composer is raised
to eloquence via his pen when considering the violins, from
which are evoked "the greatest power of expression and an
incontestable variety of different qualities of tone". The
violin is "in fact, the true female voice of the orchestra — a

voice at once passionate and chaste, heart-rending, yet soft, which can weep, sigh and lament, chant, pray and muse, or burst forth into joyous accents as none other can do".

Also feminine and delicate is the harp, especially in its highest octave, where the strings "have a delicate crystalline sound, of voluptuous freshness, which renders them fit for the expression of graceful fairy-like ideas, and for giving murmuring utterance to the sweetest secrets of smiling melodies". Berlioz devotes more space to the harp in his *Treatise* than to any other non-regular orchestral instrument, perhaps echoing an attachment to the ideal of Celtic purity in music. He certainly had much grander notions of the instrument's potential than his contemporaries, seeming to assume casually that harps could be marshalled almost like violins: "When the harps are numerous . . . . they are generally divided into firsts and seconds . . . . a still greater number of different harp-parts might doubtless be excellently employed". He also declares that "nothing can be more in keeping with ideas of poetic festivities, or religious rites, than the sound of a large body of harps ingeniously introduced".

This would be extravagant language even today, let alone in 1844; yet, characteristically, he practised what he preached by asking for twelve harps in one of his own 'religious rites': the March for the Presentation of the Colours performed as an adjunct to the *Te Deum*. He also employs six harps for climactic moments in *The Trojans*; but while we now readily accept his demand for two harps in the 'Ball' movement of the *Fantastic Symphony* (the instrument's first appearance in any symphony, incidentally), there is a temptation still to deride the idea of *twelve* (or even six) in any earthbound music. On this point, musicologist Hugh Macdonald declares: "It is *not* absurd for Berlioz to ask for twelve harps . . . . because that was the effect he wanted. Berlioz was not concerned so much with how many harpists were available . . . . as with how many were required to make that exhilarating sound; he would no more accept one or two harps as a maximum than one or two violins".[90]

Dealing with the harp when blended with other instruments, Berlioz advocates use of its harmonics with woodwind, as "nothing comes near the sonority of these mysterious notes when united to chords from flutes and clarinets playing in the same medium". He used such a combination — with violin harmonics also — in *Romeo and Juliet*. While on plucked strings, Berlioz also commends the mandolin for its special qualities, deploring the contemporary practice of ignoring Mozart's instructions in *Don Giovanni* by using a substitute guitar or plucked violin. (For serious use of the mandolin in an orchestral score we have to look to Mahler, over half a century later.) This is not to suggest that Berlioz disliked the guitar — indeed he loved the instrument and used it for his basic studies of harmony when a young man, thus helping to give his musical idiom a curious freshness and originality.

The clarinet was a particular love of Berlioz, though he takes an opportunity in the *Treatise* to praise its use by Weber for a distant, twilight sound in *Der Freischütz*. However, he caps this in his own *Lélio*, where against a clever sonic back-cloth of string tremolos, double-bass pizzicato and pianissimo harp arpeggios, the clarinetist is required to play a tune with his instrument enclosed in a leather bag, which acts as a mute. This produces a "mournful murmur . . . a half-stifled sound" suitable for the intended mood of sorrowful dejection: a melancholic state equated by Berlioz with the very intense effects produced in him by the aeolian harp. In fact the passage in question occurs in 'Aeolian Harp: Recollections', the fifth section of *Lélio* which started life as part of *The Death of Orpheus*, the cantata used for his first attempt to gain the Rome prize in the seminal year of 1827. He remained deeply attached to this piece of orchestration and went to some trouble when in Rome four years later to obtain a copy of his original score so that the short adagio which followed Orpheus' death could be absorbed into *Lélio*. He wished to do this without any changes, as he had feelings about this shimmeringly expressive piece akin to those aroused by 'Élégie'. Later, he reported that he found performances of the adagio emotionally shattering.

Emotionally disturbing in a quite different fashion is the famous passage for trombones and flutes in the *Requiem*. Here, three trombone pedal notes are played beneath a harmony of flutes in three parts, the flutes seeming to provide extreme harmonics for the trombones — with most mysterious and majestic effect. Another innovation in this mighty work is the designation of eight pairs of drums, not out of crude extravagance or for sheer loudness, but simply to facilitate, by tuning in different ways, the playing of proper chords in three, four or five parts, and to achieve an effect of close rolls.

On the bass drum, Berlioz had strong opinions — mainly *against* its use. In the *Treatise* he soundly condemns its indiscriminate employment, advocating instead that it may be "introduced in a full piece, in the midst of a large orchestra, merely to augment little by little the force of a lofty rhythm already established, and gradually reinforced by the successive entrance of groups of the most sonorous instruments. Its introduction then does wonders; the swing of the orchestra becomes one of unmeasured potency; the noise, thus disciplined, is transformed into music". Berlioz acknowledged — and used — the bass drum, *pianissimo*, united with cymbals and struck at long intervals for a 'grand and solemn' effect; and in the *Requiem* he uses it *forte* at moments of terror, but the use is always economical — never excessive.

So much for the element of timbre in instrumentation, which Berlioz regarded as a discipline, and in orchestration, which he regarded as an art. But he is also renowned for the huge resources which he regarded as necessary, ideally, not only for his own music but for that of others. His ideal orchestra comprised 467 instrumentalists, to work with a chorus of 360; but, as usual when his performing intentions are examined, one finds few obvious excesses, and in his own scores the scale is not impossible — indeed, only three of his major works need an unusually large body of players: the *Requiem*, *Te Deum* and *Funeral and Triumphal* symphony. Even in the latter, a work conceived for a public occasion in the open air, his resources are employed carefully to avoid the monotonous effect of an unremitting fortissimo. Similarly in the *Requiem*, where the hair-raising impact of multidirectional brass in the *Dies irae* is the more noticeable against the work's overall restraint. Another factor in Berlioz's seemingly over-zealous insistence on large numbers was his belief (well founded acoustically) that *quiet* passages depend for their perfection on the smoothness of tone thus achieved by the mutual cancellation of sonic irregularities.

Numbers large or small, the inveterate perfectionist also insisted on maintaining a sensible balance between instrumental families in the orchestra, protesting at the unthinking addition of brass and percussion without a corresponding increase in the string departments. He objected to the casual and conventional use of horns, trumpets, violas and bassoons simply to 'fill in' the harmony, or to thicken the texture just for the sake of thickening. He adopted a limpid, transparent scoring which lets the listener hear into the texture.

Balance of a more massive kind may be seen at work in the *Te Deum*, in which the organ is used not so much to augment the orchestra as to contrast with it, in a manner exactly as he had advocated in his *Treatise* six years before composition. As Berlioz commented, the two are to resemble "Pope and Emperor, speaking in dialogue from opposite ends of the nave". This raises the matter of space and acoustics, a topic on which his pen was also active. When over 6000 London orphans singing in St. Paul's Cathedral in 1851 had such an overwhelming effect upon him, he attributed the effect not only to the number and quality of the voices, but also "to the disposition of the singers in very high tiers. The reflectors and producers of sound are thus nicely balanced. The air within the church is struck from so many points at once, in surface and in depth, that it vibrates as a whole and its disturbance develops a power and majesty of action on the human nervous system which the most learned efforts of musical art under ordinary conditions have so far not given us any notion of."[91] One practical effect of the St. Paul's event was that Berlioz added a children's chorus (but only 600) to his own *Te Deum*, which received its first performance in 1855 to mark the opening of the Universal Exhibition in Paris. Again, a religious work for a big public occasion, though this was the only performance he ever heard.

Berlioz dearly wished to have the use of some great hall or church in Paris, with a vast acoustic like that of St. Paul's in London, and had on several occasions made unsuccessful attempts to persuade the authorities to make the Pantheon available for this purpose. Following the London event, he mused on the sort of music that might be performed by several hundred instruments and a choir of 4000 mixed voices in the Pantheon:

> A fine work, written in a style suited to such means, on a subject in which grandeur blends with nobility, and in which one is stirred by the expression of all the elevated thoughts that can move the heart of man. I believe that such a manifestation of the most powerful of the arts, aided by the magic of poetry and architecture, would

be truly worthy of a nation like ours and would leave far behind the vaunted festivals of antiquity.[92]

Though to some extent a secularised echo of an atmosphere evoked in the great Gothic cathedrals, such grandiose dreams were not to come true in France, or indeed on Earth. Only in his imaginary Euphonia, a society in which music and poetry are the whole object of existence, are there resources for such schemes. He describes there a great musical amphitheatre in which homage is paid to all things spiritual by means of mighty performances of the greatest music. In this he sums up and expands other more earth-bound projects of similar intent offered in various minor writings, prompting a suggestion by Jacques Barzun in an essay entitled *Euphonia and Bayreuth: Musical Cities* that Wagner's ideas for a great musical centre had their origin in Berlioz's speculations.[93] In any event, this is the truly romantic Berlioz, dreaming of the impossible but somehow managing to believe that creative imagination may still perform a miracle. But not for him, in his own time or country.

In a later time, we may guess from various critical remarks about excessive chromaticism in some of Wagner's music that he would have been out of sympathy with the 20th century attempts to abandon consonance as a basis of the art. In reply to a composer who had sought approval for the manner in which he had rendered the shouts of a noisy operatic crowd by means of a chorus of continuous discords, Berlioz said: "Go and invite one of your own way of thinking; order the cups of oxidised copper to be brought in; pour out your vitriol; and drink. As for me, I prefer water — even luke-warm; or even an opera of Cimarosa!"[94] Summing up a discussion of musical and unmusical principles, he brings together the arguments for proper timbre and proper harmony, both aspects of sound *as heard*:

> No doubt the exclusive object of music is not to make itself agreeable to the ear; but, still less, should its object be to be disagreeable to it; to torture and assault it. Being simply human, I desire that my sensations should be taken into account.[95]

The actual sound of music was always for him the final test, which set him against the rigid preconceptions of those "whose pride and principles were outraged by my

heterodoxy in matters of harmony and rhythm." He went on:
"I am a free-thinker in music, or rather I am of the faith of
Beethoven, Weber, Gluck and Spontini, who . . . prove by
their works that everything is 'right' or 'wrong' according to
the effects produced, and that is the sole criterion for con-
demning or exonerating any given arrangement of notes."[96]
It was this same empirical awareness of sonic effects that
made him distrustful of music which strayed too far from
the embrace of consonance. "My style is very bold" he said
"but there is no tendency in it whatsoever to destroy any of
the fundamental elements of art . . . I have never dreamed of
writing music 'without melody', as people in France have
absurdly maintained. Such a school now exists in Germany
and I abominate it."[97] Characteristically, one of the best
short summaries of his musical style came from his own pen:

> The predominant features of my music are passionate expression,
> inward intensity, rhythmic impetus, and a quality of unexpected-
> ness. When I say passionate expression, I mean an expression bent
> on reproducing the inner meaning of its subject, even when that
> subject is the opposite of passion, and gentle, tender feelings are
> being expressed, or a profound calm.[98]

The 'inner meaning' of a subject, the trick of transformation
which captured and transmuted an external impulse — be it
literary, religious, erotic or political — into a piece of self-
propelling musical imagination: this was the core of Berlioz
the composer. And he was a musician who often managed,
despite misconceptions which persist more than a century
after his death, to impose a classical restraint on the most
turbulent of feelings — to produce music of tenderness or
finesse just as masterfully as music of grandeur or terror. But
such thoughts verge onto aspects of musical aesthetics beyond
the scope of this study.

9

Intellectual At Large

Through all the disillusion and loneliness of Berlioz the composer, especially in his later years, Berlioz the intellectual remained poised and his interests and human sympathies wide. Alert to the communicative possibilities of an expanding technology, he looked with hope to the future rather than in nostalgia to the past:

> I admire our civilization more and more, with its post, telegraph, steam and electricity — slaves to the human will, which permit the more rapid transmission of thought.[99]

He was presumably in such a mood when he agreed in 1846, at very short notice, to compose music to some words by his journalist friend Jules Janin for a *Railway Cantata*, to celebrate the opening of the Northern Railway at Lille at the climax of the first (and in the event financially disastrous) French 'railway mania'. An insignificant work, the cantata nevertheless symbolised a rationalist-utilitarian attitude to material progress which contradicted that of the now aged and once admired Chateaubriand. Despite visions of a world united by transport, and poverty eliminated by science, Chateaubriand feared for men's spiritual future and declared that "No one can give life except by morality; one only succeeds in creating peoples along heaven-ways; railways will only lead us all the more swiftly to the abyss."[100]

In this more romantically pessimistic vein, Berlioz is on another occasion openly ironic about 'progress', referring contemptuously to the fact that next year's peaches will be as large as this year's melons. The difference in attitude may arise from the unexpected twists of a complex personality, but also possibly from the fact that one improvement concerns mind and the other matter — thoughts and peaches. This is crucial, for Berlioz always sought or admired elevated spiritual states and welcomed the meeting of minds concerned with beauty or with ultimate things. "We discussed art, poetry, philosophy, music and drama — in a word all that constitutes life",[101] he wrote to his sister in 1834, and such discussions retained a crucial chordal significance in the quick-silver polyphony of his mental life. In a vein of slight self-mockery in the last Roman chapter of his *Memoirs*, Berlioz describes a pretentious quartet of students (of which he was one) concerned to:

> extend and perfect the grand new system of philosophy . . . . known as the 'System of Absolute Indifference in all that pertains to Matter', a transcendental doctrine which aims to produce in man the sensitivity and rounded perfection of a stone. Our system does not catch on. Objections are raised: the existence of pain and pleasure, feelings, sensations. We are regarded as mad . . . . we are simply laughed at. Great philosophers have always been misunderstood.[102]

Is this simply the mature man looking back at a piece of youthful naïvety, or is it Berlioz the rational observing Berlioz the romantic? Certainly the two facets of his mind wove a never-ending counterpoint in the texture of his personality, as also in his music. The lightly humorous touch evident here also infiltrated his thoughts on other topics, sometimes providing a veneer for surprisingly obscure corners of knowledge. He once made a joke, for instance, of the fact that Roger and Francis Bacon could not be related because Roger the celibate Friar would have had no offspring. Berlioz seemed here to take it for granted that French readers of music criticism would know of these English pioneers of scientific method and empirical philosophy from the 13th and 16th centuries, though it is unlikely that they would have heard even of Locke and Hume.

A quite remarkable rational detachment is often found in his extensive writings on music. His criticism published in *Journal des Débats*, *Gazette Musicale* and other papers would fill many volumes. Indeed, for long periods it seemed to his French contemporaries that he was primarily a critic and only incidentally a composer, as also with Schumann in

Germany, who must be coupled with Berlioz as one of the founders of modern music criticism — both of them in a composer/critic tradition originated by Weber and Hoffmann. Also, outside France Berlioz was renowned as much for his conducting and his pioneer performances of Beethoven's symphonies, as for his compositions. Though much of his writing work was a drudgery — a fact that Berlioz took every opportunity to mention — he maintained a striking ability to couple artistic enthusiasms or depressions with crystal-clear logic and an elegant wit.

He also disciplined himself against personal feelings which might colour artistic judgement: "I can no more prevent myself from admiring a sublime work by my greatest enemy than from loathing the nonsense of my most intimate friend".[103] Thus he praised Mendelssohn's music even though this erstwhile friend of Roman days did little to disguise a distaste for Berlioz's work. He wrote a fair-minded and appreciative obituary on Cherubini, who as Director of the Conservatoire had been his great enemy in student days. Also, while he disliked Italian music in general and Rossini in particular, he gave credit where he thought it due — to *William Tell*, *Le Comte Ory* and *The Barber of Seville*.

Although he never founded a musicological or aesthetic 'school', much of his writing concerned the untapped possibilities of music. Yet despite his almost religious devotion to the idea of music as a sort of all-embracing poetry of the spirit, the rational empiricist lurks in another corner of his mind, and suddenly we find him writing in a mood of reasoning, analytical calmness. Thus in a note discussing supposedly descriptive elements in his music:

> The composer knows quite well that music is a substitute neither for speech nor for the art of drawing. He has never had the absurd pretension of reproducing abstract ideas or moral qualities, but only passions and impressions; nor has he ever entertained the even stranger notion of depicting mountains: he has only wished to reproduce the melodic style and forms of singing common among certain mountain populations, while at the same time imparting the emotion felt by the soul in certain circumstances at the sight of those imposing heights.[104]

This coolly detached Berlioz, asked by an admirer to state his aesthetic creed, replied disarmingly: "My aesthetic is in my

works, in what I have done and what I have not done".[105]
He went even further in apparent denial of a faith which
sometimes illuminated his whole life:

> The question of what is beautiful would . . . . seem to be a question
> of time and place. A sad conclusion, but true. For unless absolute
> beauty is that which at all times, in all places, and by all men must
> be acknowledged as beautiful, I cannot imagine what it means or
> where it might reside. And that kind of beauty I am sure does not
> exist. I believe only that there exist artistic beauties of which the
> appreciation has become inherent in certain civilizations and which
> will last, thanks to a minority, as long as those civilizations them-
> selves.[106]

In the context of a Romanticism in revolt against the rule-
bound certainties of Enlightenment aesthetics, this declaration
is not so calmly 'rational' as one might think, despite Berlioz's
clarity of expression. The ascription of beauty to civilisation
and a minority of men rather than to an objective pattern of
natural law discoverable by reason is in some respects a piece
of romantic radicalism. It is in the tradition of Victor Hugo's
Preface to *Cromwell*, an influential manifesto of 1827 which
summed up a mood of mounting discontent with a conservative neoclassicism in the arts, and paved the way (as did
Shakespeare's plays around the same time) for Hugo's own
Hernani in 1830. The revolution of that year inspired the
painter Eugène Delacroix to produce his popular *Liberty
Leading the People* — perhaps the closest parallel in the arts
to Berlioz leading a Parisian crowd singing the *Marseillaise* —
while Delacroix's own utterances on visual aesthetics sometimes echoed the composer's philosophy just quoted. Thèo-
phile Gautier, whose verses Berlioz used in *Nuit d'Été*, noted
in the daily paper *La Presse* that "with Victor Hugo and
Eugène Delacroix, Hector Berlioz appears to us to form the
Trinity of Romantic Art".[107]

Despite this and their similar ages, and notwithstanding a
common respect for Beethoven, a shared passion for Shakespeare and (for Berlioz and Delacroix) Byron and Goethe,
with the same sort of battle to be fought for a changing art,
the only notable appreciation for *each other's* work among
the three was that of Berlioz for Hugo. Although conceding
that Beethoven was perhaps a man with a message worth
studying, Delacroix condemned both Hugo and Berlioz for

raising hopes of the impossible. He reacted to a concert which included a Beethoven overture and Berlioz's *Damnation of Faust* by declaring that "the *Leonora* overture seemed as confused as before . . . and the same applies to the Berlioz. It's an appalling din, a kind of heroic hotch-potch".[108] The artist who was renowned for ignoring classical conventions when applying paint to canvas, and who declared that the finest works of art are those which follow the untramelled fantasies of the creator, deplored a similar ethos when applied to music.

Berlioz, however, had no strong feelings about painters or painting, his references to the subject usually occurring as asides in a musical context. Thus Ingres, arch-enemy of Romanticism, gets a favourable mention because he happened to share the composer's admiration for Gluck and his dislike of Rossinian fripperies. The supreme colorist in sound who acknowledged that "instrumentation is, in music, the exact equivalent of colour in painting",[109] had no more than a passing interest in the visual arts of his own time, though he paid lip-service to great creations of the past. Berlioz casually remarked, for instance, that in a production of Gluck's opera *Orphée* the graceful attitudes of the singer Pauline Viardot "recall those of certain characters in the landscapes of Poussin; or, rather, certain bas-reliefs that Poussin took for his models".[110] Also, of Beethoven's *Pastoral Symphony*, that "this astonishing landscape seems as if it were the joint work of Poussin and Michelangelo",[111] implying that all cultivated people would be familiar with these masters. But his real enthusiasm here was for Beethoven's direct evocation of landscape itself:

> that light! — that eloquent silence! that vast horizon! — those enchanted nooks secreted in the woods! — those golden harvests! — those rose-tinted clouds like wandering flecks upon the surface of the sky! — that immense plain seeming to slumber beneath the rays of the mid-day sun![112]

This fond vision of a pre-romantic landscape, grand in scale yet calmly 'classical' in the manner of the countryside of his childhood, should not really have been confessed by the careful rationalist who had denied that music can represent such things!

The romantic in him also loved the more turbulent scenery

which inspired so many painters in his time, particularly 'apocalyptic' artists such as John Martin, whose visionary pictures were very popular in France. Heine once embarrassed Berlioz by suggesting that his music paralleled the excesses of Martin's grandiose 'Babylonian' paintings — a rather extreme view tending to encourage the false notion that his compositions are nothing if not massive. More recently it has been claimed that some of Berlioz's music depicting diabolical scenes was suggested by the work of Martin, as he once made an imaginative reference to the painter's picture of pandemonium; but evidence of a causal connection seems rather slight.[113] Berlioz was certainly exposed to paints and canvas in a most favourable manner during his stay in Italy, where the Director of the French Academy was the noted painter Horace Vernet, whom he liked. But as he made no more than an occasional passing reference to painters or paintings in later life, we must assume at least a temperamental neutrality on the subject.

Architecture sometimes impressed him, especially buildings with historical associations. He loved St. Peter's in Rome and was especially stirred by the churches of Moscow. Writing to Prince Odoevsky a year before his death, recalling their happy talks when he had visited Russia, Berlioz effused:

> Think about your Hector when you look across Red Square at the ancient Church of Ivan the Terrible; remember how his soul was shaken by the beauty of what he saw. . . . . My soul sings when I think about that unforgettable city where I saw reflected the stirring events of past ages. When I visited Rome and Florence I experienced a similar feeling, but there it didn't seize me with the same warmth which I felt on becoming acquainted with Moscow while in your company and falling in love with the blue and gold domes of your churches.[114]

Although he qualified his enthusiasm in the reference to Italy, Berlioz's memory had perhaps become slightly rose-tinted in the course of 37 years. In a letter from Rome written in 1831 when he was friendly with Mendelssohn, he said that his fellow composer "would take me to see all the famous ruins which, I confess, did not move me very much."[115] But if his response to man-made visual beauty was variable, his love of the sights and sounds of 'nature in the raw' never flagged: landscapes and seascapes alike had a tonic effect, to which he returned for spiritual refreshment.

Sitting in a tower at Nice during one such break in 1844, he composed the salty, buccaneering *Corsaire* overture which, though for a while named *Le Corsaire Rouge* in fond memory of a childhood reading of Fenimore Cooper's *The Red Rover*, was eventually given its Byronic connotation. Although the work probably had roots in his own first experience *on* the sea when crossing from Marseilles to Leghorn on the way to Rome in 1831, he really was greatly stirred by Byron's pirate. He relates in the *Memoirs* how he would take a volume of poetry to read in the cool of St. Peter's in Rome, where he became absorbed in the 'burning verse' of *The Corsair*. The connection between Byron and his own little nautical adventure, which happened to involve a lively storm, was probably cemented in his mind by the boastings of a crew member who claimed to have commanded Byron's boat during the Greek expedition, navigating it through an even fiercer storm whilst playing cards with the great man himself.

Byron was a member of that 'minority' referred to by Berlioz as the custodians of civilization, and as they seem to have played such a large part in his thoughts — and some of them in his music — they will introduce the next chapter.

10

Influences and Attitudes

The poetic idealists who fight the good fight in an uncomprehending world — spiritual 'outsiders' in whose illustrious
company Berlioz placed himself — continually stoked the
fires of his own creativity. He was both a lamp of originality
and a mirror, through his music, to the genius of others.
These others were mostly creators, like the lone artist-hero in
his opera *Benvenuto Cellini*. Cellini was a 16th century Italian
sculptor, goldsmith and shamelessly infamous adventurer
whose autobiography Berlioz read in 1833. Benvenuto's
brushes with philistinism and established authority struck a
sympathetic chord with the composer, who honoured him
by devoting much of the first chapter of *Evenings with the
Orchestra* to a fictitious correspondence between a thinly
disguised Berlioz and a heavily white-washed Cellini. Also, in
his *Memoirs* Berlioz equated the 16th century persecutions
and indignities suffered by the goldsmith with the 19th century neglect of Adolphe Sax.

But Berlioz's greatest homage was the opera, composed in
the 1830s to a libretto by Barbier and Wailly. It is a work of
astonishing beauties and subtleties — an interplay of music
and life packed with humour and rare adventure, evoking
the creative explosion and tumult of existence that we know
as the Italian Renaissance. One wonders whether Alexandre
Dumas (the elder) had come across Berlioz's *Benvenuto Cellini* when he wrote his novel *Ascanio* in 1843, as this portrays
Cellini within a remarkably similar plot. But Dumas' story is
one of a vast outpouring of historical novels mostly forgotten — as is Saint-Saens' opera *Ascanio*, partly derived from

Dumas' book — whereas the Berlioz work shines more bright-
ly than ever, a mirror reflecting the cutting intensity of the
composer's original feelings about the sculptor.

Similar feelings could be stirred by thoughts of any great
pioneer of the mind, whether artist or explorer. Thus he was
affected by the very name of Christopher Columbus and
angered to find that the city of Genoa had erected no monument to its son who discovered the New World. Perhaps he
had this Italian insult to genius in mind when commissioning
the verses for his *Romeo and Juliet*, wherein Friar Laurence
declares that the city of Verona will one day be remembered
solely for its connection with the tragic couple:

> Poor children, for whom I weep,
> Struck down together before your time,
> On your tragic resting-place
> Posterity will come to weep.
> Famous through you in history
> Verona one day unwittingly
> Will find her sorrow and her glory
> In your memory alone.

A touching ideological variation on Shakespeare, whose nearest approach to this is found in the words of Montague:

> For I will raise her statue in pure gold;
> That while Verona by that name is known,
> There shall no figure at such rate be set
> As that of true and faithful Juliet.

The creative artist especially was for him a hero, whether
poet, writer, painter or sculptor. "The great musicians share
the fate of almost all humanity's pioneers"[116] wrote Berlioz,
who then proceeded to argue his case with the examples of
Beethoven, Mozart, Shakespeare, Cervantes, Tasso and Camoens. This last was a 16th century poet, lover, adventurer,
soldier and traveller-to-the-Orient, who — no doubt signifi-
cantly for Berlioz — had been called the Virgil of Portugal.
The Romantic in him tended to believe that man's highest
creations would always go unheeded in their own time, that
true art could only triumph in some later age. This side of
Berlioz echoed Shelley, who had declared in his *Defence of
Poetry* that poetry "acts in a divine and unapprehended
manner, beyond and above consciousness; and it is reserved

for future generations . . . . a poet is a nightingale, who sits in
darkness and sings to cheer its own solitude with sweet
sounds".

But the more practical Berlioz would sometimes concede
that the artist's life was not universally tragic, and that ordinary workaday human weaknesses rather than implacable fate
might on occasion account for adverse reactions to new
creations. In this more pragmatic vein he related the guarded
response of his teacher, the composer Lesueur, to a performance of Beethoven's fifth symphony in 1828. Lesueur, who
was helpful to Berlioz at the Conservatoire, had admitted
being moved by the work but nevertheless declared that
"music like that ought not to be written". "Poor human
nature!" says Berlioz, "Poor master! What a world of regret,
of stubborn resentment, jealousy, dread of the unknown,
confession of incapacity lies behind it and all such remarks
made by countless men in similar situations!"[117]

But 'countless men' was not all men, and not all creativity
worthy of veneration was located safely in the past. Neither
did all artists fail to achieve due recognition, or at least spasmodic triumphs, in their own time — facts which the rational
Berlioz carefully noted. One such triumph was Flaubert's
novel *Salammbô* which inspired Berlioz, aged 59, to declare
to its author: it "has filled me with admiration, wonder and
even terror . . . . What a style! What archaeological knowledge! I say your mysterious Salammbô, with her secret
unwilling love, mixed with repulsion, for the enemy who has
violated her, is a creation of highest poetry and at the same
time wholly within the bounds of veritable truth."[118] Poetry
and truth in an antique setting — here indeed was a kindred
spirit at work.

Flaubert was poised ambivalently between Romanticism
and Realism in literature, he was fascinated by the past as a
mixture of myth and history, and he hated the bourgeois
mentality; exchange literature for music and this could be
Berlioz. Flaubert came to appreciate their natural affinity
only some years after Berlioz's death, when, on reading some
of the composer's published correspondence, he wrote to his
niece: "Read it, I beg you. There was a man! And a true
artist! . . . . It surpasses the correspondence of Balzac by
thirty-six thousand arms' lengths! I am no longer surprised
at the sympathy there was between us. If only I had known

him better! I would have loved him!"[119]

Many years earlier, in the public setting of a controversy about *Hernani*, Berlioz's enthusiasm had been for Hugo. This underlines an important fact: he kept in touch with the literary and intellectual life of his contemporaries to an extent almost unparalleled amongst major composers. While his loyalties were sometimes determined by purely musical considerations – as when he praised Pushkin not for his writings but because the Russian liked Weber's *Der Freischütz* – he did have many genuine devotions.

A fair number of such interests found their way into his music as sources for ideas or words. Even the *Fantastic Symphony*, that supposedly most 'autobiographical' of works, had twin literary roots. When prescribing the programme for his symphony – an 'Episode in the Life of an Artist' – Berlioz cited Chateaubriand's melancholy, world-weary René as the prototype for the subject of his imaginings. The *René* story, whose partner *Atala* Berlioz hoped for a while to make the basis of an opera, could itself be traced back through a tradition of personal outpourings, stemming from Rousseau's *Confessions* and lodged as isolated pre-romantic gems within the rather dull neoclassical literary fabric of Napoleonic France. Outside France a parallel tone had been set many years before by Goethe's *Sufferings of the Young Werther*, but it was not until the cultural upheaval of the 1820s that France re-joined what had become the romantic mainstream elsewhere, and her sons fell victim to the 'spleen' of which Berlioz complained so vehemently. This introspective melancholy, the *mal du siècle** which sometimes seemed like a flamboyant fashion rather than a genuine cultural phenomenon, echoed the *Weltschmerz* which arose in Germany as an aspect of 'Wertherism' and hovered in France as an example for some of Berlioz's more egocentric poses.

The other 'confession' behind Berlioz's first symphony was Alfred de Musset's youthful and very free translation of De Quincy's *Confessions of an English Opium Eater*, which he read in 1829. The connection here is quite direct: not only is it likely that the composer tried opium himself (at least experimentally) as a result of reading the book, but his music reflects some of De Quincy's and Musset's visions almost

*malady of the century

literally — particularly the haunting figure of a girl whose
reappearances bring an uneasy sense of doom. She was
immortalised by Berlioz's *idée fixe* phrase which troubles "a
young musician of morbid disposition and powerful imagination" who, having taken opium, is plunged "into a deep sleep
accompanied by strange dreams in which sensations, feelings
and memories are transformed in his sick brain into musical
images and ideas". Later, when Musset reached the age at
which Berlioz had composed the *Fantastic Symphony* (and
after a famous and chaotic affair with George Sand) he
delivered his own *Confession of a Child of the Century*. This
high watermark of self-regarding anguish, the lonely ennui of
romantic youth and love's jealousies, could be said to occupy
the position in French literature (or the position which its
title suggests it should have) that the *Fantastic Symphony*
has in Western music.

The literary connections of Berlioz's other major works
are: Shakespeare, *Romeo & Juliet* and *Beatrice & Benedict*;
Virgil, *The Trojans*; Byron, *Harold in Italy*; Goethe, *Damnation of Faust*; Cellini, *Benvenuto Cellini*; Moore, *Irlande*; and
Gautier, *Nuits d'Été*. To these may be added the *Requiem*
and *Te Deum* (Catholic liturgy) and *Infant Christ* (Bible). If
we consider the whole range of compositions with literary
sources beyond his own writings (excluding the work of
translators or versifiers following his instructions) the list
breaks down as follows: Shakespeare (8); Catholic liturgy
(5); Moore and Hugo (3 each); Goethe, Byron, Scott, Gautier,
Béranger, Brizeux, Vieillard (2 each); Virgil, Aquinas, Cellini,
Chateaubriand, Herder, De Quincy, Tasso, Lamartine, Dumas,
Ferrand, Barbier, Deschamps, Beauvoir, Leuven, Vaudin,
Du Boys, Guérin, Janin, Bible (one each).

These are sources used in his music, though numerous
quotations and references in his writings indicate a lively
interest in literature generally. In addition to the 28 authors
listed above, a round-up of all those other writers who influenced, inspired or entertained Berlioz in some form at some
time — apart from in medical and musical textbooks — gives
the following list of 32 more: Alfieri, Balzac, Beccaria, Boileau, Bossuet, Bougainville, Cabanis, Camoens, Cervantes,
Corneille, D'Ortigue, De Vigny, Euripides, Fenimore Cooper,
Flaubert, Florian, Gall, Heine, Hoffmann, Horace, La Fontaine, Lamennais, Lebrun, Livy, Lucan, Molière, Ovid, Racine,

Rousseau, Saint-Pierre, Schiller and Voltaire.

A very mixed bag, the last two perhaps symbolising as well as any the German/romantic and French/rationalist strands in his own outlook, and the ardour trimmed with logic which was the hallmark of his own writing. He was very conscious of literary style in others, and sometimes rather critical of verbal shortcomings: "nothing being more odious . . . . than that ambiguous style, the pretended depth of which is designed not so much for the purpose of veiling the author's thought, and of rendering its perception difficult, as to conceal the fact that he has no thought worth mentioning".[120]

As we have seen, his own descriptive powers were by no means confined to purely musical matters. His letters and countless critical articles, the *Memoirs*, *Treatise*, *Evenings* and various collections of essays (most notably *Les Grotesques de la Musique* and *A Travers Chants**) reveal an active and widely interested mind — a mind alert to parallels and analogies stretching across normally unconnected subjects. In describing the ordered manner in which the orphaned children took their places from the top of the cathedral downwards when preparing for the 1851 St. Paul's concert which so impressed him, Berlioz drew upon physics and chemistry. The process "presented an unusual spectacle which suggested what occurs in the microscopic world during the phenomenon of crystallization. The shafts of this crystal made up of human molecules that continually proceeded from the circumference to the centre, were of two colours: the dark blue coats of the small boys on the upper tiers and the white gowns and caps of the little girls in the lower rows."[121]

Here was a mind also not averse to a little futuristic fantasy, as in the tale of Euphonia. Jules Verne, who shot to fame soon after Berlioz died, would never have made the composer's mistake of placing the city five whole centuries hence; but Berlioz did at least assume that aerial transport had revolutionised the world. He also anticipated mid-20th century education by describing in 1844 a system of bodily exercise to music remarkably like modern eurhythmics. Such fantasy, likely to come true, arose from a nice blend of romance and rationality congenial to Berlioz's nature.

***Musical Curiosities** and *In Realms of Song*

Not so congenial to him was the craze for table-turning Spiritualism, popularized in France by Allan Kardec, which swept from North America to Europe in the 1850s following the mysterious experiences of the Fox family near New York in 1848. In particular, it was claimed that the spirit of Beethoven, with which Berlioz of all people would dearly have loved to commune, was manifesting itself at seances. But he would have none of it, and brought some gentle scorn to bear on the subject in an essay entitled *Beethoven in the Ring of Saturn*:

> The poor spirits, we must admit, are very obedient. Beethoven, whilst he was on earth, would not have put himself out of the way to go even from the Carinthian Gate to the Imperial Palace even if the Emperor of Austria had sent to beg him urgently to come. And now he quits Saturn's ring, and interrupts his high contemplations to obey the *order* (mark the word) of the very first comer who only happens to be possessed of a deal table. See the effect of death and how that changes your character.[122]

Perhaps in these days of carefully tabulated physical research and the emergence of University Chairs in parapsychology, Berlioz would be more wary. He would surely at least have been intrigued to learn that a century after his death a notable medium would claim to be in occasional contact with *him*,[123] or that the present author would speculate on possible psychic factors behind his interest in Ireland and Robert Emmet (see Appendix). But the mocking, sceptical side of his nature dominated in such matters, to be paralleled by an ironic incredulity towards fairy tales from the past. Referring to the legend of music from a Confucian ivory-inlaid guitar said to have been used to improve the morals of ancient China, Berlioz indicated a desire to know more of the instrument:

> being as I am, a guitar player myself, yet never having so much as improved the morals of the population of a small bedroom (far from it). My guitar . . . . is rude and simple . . . . had it only been ornamented with ivory, think of the benefits I might have brought, the heresies I might have rooted out, the truths instilled, the noble religion founded, and the happiness we might all be enjoying now. It seems hardly possible that such calamity should come simply for want of a strip of ivory.[124]

For the Romantics, an incapacity for faith (or superstition) was a challenge to create a new undogmatic religion. But while their movement was in some ways a Germanic revolt of the spirit against the static, elegant world of 18th century French rationalism, Berlioz's sceptical bent prevented him from wallowing in the mystical transcendentalism which eventually came to dominate German romantic philosophy. Thus in his *Damnation of Faust* the dreamer is actually damned — not saved by the final miracle propounded in Goethe's *Faust* Part 2. Berlioz hesitated momentarily over this and included a brief hint of possible salvation in his first performing text; but this was scrapped and Faust descended thereafter to eternal agony.

This seems to be an anti-romantic gesture, a stoic declaration that the questing spirit might be condemned to its own hell of isolation, a hell which afflicted Berlioz himself with increasing pain after the total failure of his *Faust* at its first performance in 1846. But lonely melancholy was also a romantic trait, and an alternative view is that this very pessimism is the more truly romantic in spirit. On this inter-pretation, Goethe's long delayed second part to the poem was really a weak concession to the humanitarian sentiments of Enlightenment philosophy. Earlier versions of the Faust story all condemned the philosopher to hellfire, and as the complex web of German piety, superstitions and 'mysteries' which nurtured the legend was one of the fountain-heads of Romanticism itself, it has been argued that Berlioz was simply opting for a more genuinely rounded story than that offered by Goethe.[125] The German poet had never really grasped the subterranian rumblings tapped by a Roman-ticism which he had reluctantly helped to launch in his youth and from which he withdrew in his maturity.

Although he produced his early *Eight Scenes* before Goethe had started writing Part 2, Berlioz almost certainly knew of the poet's sentimental finale by the time he was working on the *Damnation*. Goethe's deviation from the older tradition was criticised by George Sand and Berlioz's friend Heine, among others. Also, the French version of *Faust* Part 1 by Gérard de Nerval on which the composer drew was commonly coupled with a translation of *Lenore*, a fantasy by the pre-romantic German G.A. Bürger. Significant-ly, this included a Faust-like 'compact' and ride to the abyss much closer in spirit to Berlioz's pessimistic version than anything to be found in Goethe.[126]

But the pessimist in Berlioz was an evil spirit over whom he triumphed in many battles, rising to the challenge of his own unbelief with his own faith. In this secular religion he worshipped a god of Creation compounded of the holy trinity, Music, Love and Poetry, with bourgeois philistinism playing the part of Satan — a devil nevertheless often all to frequently successful in driving him to the verge of nihilistic despair.

11

Slaying the Philistine Devil

The complacent bourgeois ethos which Berlioz so despised, an unimaginative philistinism which expected Art to entertain, never to elevate, was so often in his thoughts that it deserves at least this short chapter to itself. Then we can attempt a final assault on the summit of his artistic faith.

The composer's private Devil is best introduced by an episode in his Italian sojourn, as described in the *Memoirs*. He is sitting in St. Peter's in Rome, "so vast, so nobly beautiful, so serene and majestic", indulging a private reverie on his hero Byron, who had been before him in this very place. He speculates on one who had been "so profoundly loved. Yes, loved, a poet, free, rich". He feels frustrated at the thought, and in such a mood he observes a peasant who

> came in and, going quietly up, kissed St. Peter's big toe. Lucky creature, I thought with bitterness, what do you lack? You believe, you have hope . . . . When you go out of here, what will you be looking for? A patch of shade to sleep in . . . . What are your dreams of wealth? The handful of piastres necessary to buy a donkey or get married . . . . What is a wife in your eyes? An object of a different sex. What do you ask of art? That it give tangible form to the gods you worship, make you laugh, and provide something to dance to. For you, painting means the Virgin in red and green; drama means puppets and Punch and Judy; music means the bagpipe and the tambourine — whereas for me it means resentment and despair, because I lack everything that I am looking for and have no hope of finding it.[127]

Here, in a series of negatives, we see reflected the ideal world of his dreams. In this world he would, like Byron, be loved;

he would neither waste his time sleeping in patches of shade nor his wealth on donkeys and social trappings; his wife would share passions other than sex, and art would be something greater than a titivator of the senses or mere clothing for superstition; painting would be a gateway to new perceptions and drama a passport to all the turmoils and aspirations of the human spirit; music would be an expression of the inexpressible through every instrumental and vocal means knowable to man. But at the moment thoughts of music bring 'resentment and despair': Berlioz is suffering from his recurrent acute sense of isolation, for in Rome there is no musical life and his frustration echoes the perennial battle between unsatisfied creativity and empty contentment.

France took the brunt of his attacks on a commercially busy but aesthetically dead society, but as an admirer of Gluck, legendary critic of Italian opera, he was predisposed to regard Italy as the source of all that was trivial in music. This tended to become an antipathy towards Italian life in general and was sometimes stretched to the point of an irrational xenophobia of the sort he normally despised. From the safe fictional confines of his essay on Euphonia he regaled Italy, a land "formerly so rich in poets, painters and musicians, this soil which after Greece was the second great temple of art, where the people themselves had a feeling for it, where eminent artists were honoured almost as much as they are today in northern Europe, you see nothing but factories, workshops, mills, markets, warehouses, workers of every sex and age, burning with the thirst for gold and the fever of cupidity."[128]

In this negative reaction he was at odds with many of his fellow-Romantics: Goethe, Turner, Stendhal, Byron, Shelley, Heine, Flaubert and a host of others were inspired by their 'discovery' of the Mediterranean and Italy. Yet Berlioz scoffed at Stendhal for attending the Roman Carnival which he had found so nauseating in 1831, and which Goethe had loved many years before. Presumably he could not have agreed with his admired Byron, who saw irresistable beauty even in decay:

> Thou art the garden of the world, the home
> Of all Art yields, and Nature can decree;
> Even in thy desert, what is like to thee?

Thy very weeds are beautiful, thy waste
More rich than other climes' fertility;
Thy wreck a glory, and thy ruin graced
With an immaculate charm which cannot be defaced.

Here speaks Childe Harold, and, to be fair, we should note that Berlioz did love the Italian landscape and the peasant people he met during his long tramps through the Abbruzi mountains in 1831. Despite earlier and rather different plans for some of the musical ideas involved, Berlioz eventually immortalised this rural Italy in his own Byronic reverie: *Harold in Italy*. In making Childe Harold the unifying thread of his 'Italian' symphony Berlioz was in one sense a typical product of his age, for this was one of the most widely read poems of the day. Its melancholy wanderer in a mountainous landscape traversed by pilgrims and brigands provided an attractive image to focus the romantic feelings of literate Europe. Also, the air of defiant superiority which Byron sometimes gives to Harold probably appealed to the more earnestly Germanic type of Romantic in Berlioz, and to his own sense of artistic isolation:

He who ascends to mountain-tops, shall find
The loftiest peaks most wrapt in clouds and snow;
He who surpasses or subdues mankind,
Must look down on the hate of those below.

While Berlioz commonly enough looked down on a sea of 'hate' in his own country, his attitude to France was sometimes ambivalent. He always despised its musical conservatism and regretted its unstable politics, but occasionally he conceded its superiority in the world of thought. But only occasionally, for while once it was "a hotbed of ideas . . . . How they tear the universe to pieces . . . . How they dance on the pin-point of a good phrase!",[129] on another occasion it was "a nation which has ceased to be interested in the higher manifestation of the mind; whose only god is the golden calf. The Parisians have become a barbarian people. In scarcely one rich house in ten will you find a library . . . . Execrable novels hired from the circulating library . . . . are sufficient to satisfy the general appetite for literature . . . . we are witnessing the triumph of industrialism in Art, raised to power by the crude popular instincts to which it panders, and trampling with brutish contempt on the values it has dethroned".[130]

He refused to have his own art dethroned, and conducted a life-long campaign aimed at generating greater respect for music from both public and performers. In the opera-house, especially, he was angered and frustrated by an outlook which attached more importance to prima donnas than to poetry, or which treated the theatre as an assembly for social chatter rather than as a temple for music and drama. This problem is still with us more than a century after his death, but if we are a little more respectful now it is due in no small measure to the ripples of influence radiated by Berlioz's own tough idealism. He noted that at the more serious operatic productions discussion in the foyer would not be about the work in hand, but "about the races at the Champ de Mars; of table-turning; or of the success of Tamberlick in London . . . . of the last hospital built by Jenny Lind; of the spring and of the state of the country".[131] The disrespect implied by indiscriminate applause also raised his ire, as did the 'claqueurs' who "applaud to such an extent that never, during the whole time that Mozart's *Don Giovanni* has been performed in France, has it been ever possible to hear the beautiful instrumental phrase which concludes the mask-trio; for the applause always drowns it".[132]

He went on to note that in Germany there were no such problems, and described with amazement and approval a performance of *Fidelio* he had attended in Frankfurt, where the audience remained silent right through the opera but applauded tumultuously at the end. Some of the same German seriousness joined a disdain for Parisian theatre-managers in his reaction to a ballet on the Faust story, even though he had at one time considered composing such a ballet himself:

> The idea of making Faust dance is perhaps the most prodigious which ever entered into the brainless heads of those men-of-every trade who profane everything without meaning the least harm; just as the blackbirds and sparrows in our public gardens make perches of the finest statuary.[133]

One wonders if Berlioz had come across Heine's scenario *Doktor Faust* (a 'poem for dancing' in which Mephistopheles is a woman!) or whether he would have regarded Prokofiev's wonderful *Romeo and Juliet* ballet as an insult to the genius of Shakespeare. But here he was dealing with 'brainless sparrows', impresarios who were not to be trusted an inch. The same attitude applied to singers who expected music to serve them, not *vice versa* — they caused Berlioz to declare that "Operas should not be written for singers; but singers, on the contrary, trained for operas".[134] But musicians in Paris rarely seemed to be trained adequately for his own operas, and in reply to a suggestion that *The Trojans* be revived in circumstances likely to be disastrous, he replied:

> I cannot and will not have anything to do with the world of impresarios, directors, business men, shopkeepers — all the innumerable varieties of grocer disguised under different names.[135]

The 'grocer' mentality was also attacked in *Lélio*, where Berlioz used the anonymous narrator as his mouthpiece for some propaganda. He first tackled those who, not long before, had been wont to dismiss Shakespeare as a barbarian; but he forgives them for thus "echoing the sentiments of a few soulless writers" (who happened to include Voltaire), remarking that these are not the worst opponents of genius, "for even they awaken some day and become enlightened". The real enemies for Lélio were:

> the inhabitants of the temple of jogtrotting, easy-going tradition, fanatic priests, who would sacrifice to their idiotic divinity all the most sublime ideas of our time .... Those young theorists of eighty, who wallow in a sea of prejudice, and believe that the world ceases with the shores of their islands; those old libertines of all ages, who expect music to charm, flatter, divert and caress them; denying the chaste muse all possibility of aspiring to a higher, a nobler mission. But still worse are those who dare to lay their desecrating hands upon our masterpieces, and to call their horrible mutilations by the name of improvements, for which, as they say, good taste is required. Curses upon them! They degrade Art to a miserable farce; they commit an outrage upon her.

In such situations of outrage the artist must find his joy in a creativity which is inevitably misunderstood by a flippant public — a public inclined to "play round success, like so many lambs". "It is just this playfulness which is most to be feared" wrote Berlioz, comparing French audiences with the great crowds who were said to have listened in reverent silence to Sophocles at ancient Olympic gatherings: "Were I a

Sophocles, I should prefer to see Mount Athos remain firm and cold before me, deaf to all my conjurations; rather than to be the centre of the joyous dances of a troop of Parisian lambs".[136] His stoic/romantic creed for all artists facing philistine indifference or misinterpretation was spelt out as follows:

> All that remains . . . . to compensate artists who produce their works with so much labour, and without thinking of their commercial value, is the inner satisfaction afforded by their conscience and the profound joy which they experience in measuring the amount of their progress on the road to the beautiful.[137]

To a young American composer who wrote seeking advice and support, he followed this doctrine and preached uncompromising idealism in the face of misunderstanding, saying of music:

> Yes, love it, with that great *love* which is the quintessence of the noblest passions of the human heart. One must therefore scorn the mob and its prejudices, set no store by success if it is purchased by cowardly concessions, and keep carefully out of reach of fools and madmen, and the sophists who are able to make folly look like reason.[138]

This is tough talk for private consumption, nicely balanced in the *Memoirs* by a sardonic eulogy of the 'people' as a fount of wisdom in the arts:

> How right they are, the great critics, when they say, Art is for all. If Raphael painted his divine madonnas, it was because he understood the exalted passions of the masses for the pure, the beautiful, the ideal. If Michelangelo wrested his immortal Moses from the bowels of the marble and raised up with his mighty hands a glorious temple, it was of course to satisfy their souls' yearning for profound emotions. It was to feed the sacred flame which burns in the hearts of the people that Tasso and Dante sang. Let all works not admired by the mob be anathema![139]

So far had he travelled from his Saint-Simonian youth, when such an utterance might well have been made in naïve sincerity.

12

A Secular Holy Trinity

Of the triple rock that did remain secure in Berlioz's spiritual world, it will be well to take first the delicate threads of personal love. These spanned his life from Estelle Duboeuf when he was only twelve to this same woman as the old lady Madame Fornier fifty years later, with important consequences in his artistic ideology. That first love was perfect and chaste, with such a profound impact that he was forever burdened with an impossible ideal of womanhood, an ideal which he tended to impose on his real human loves — not always to their advantage.

When the young pianist Camille Moke abandoned him for Pleyel the piano maker while he was in Rome, Berlioz enacted the most extraordinary melodramatic farce imaginable, complete with attempted suicide and endeavours to return to Paris disguised as a woman in order to commit the classic *crime passionel.* He describes this episode with detached wit in the *Memoirs*, but it cut deeply enough for him to punish Camille, lightly disguised as Ellimac, vicariously but viciously in his tale of Euphonia. (This was in the first edition; later she became Mina.) For posterity there was a creative rider to this story, for in a mood of great emotional relief after accepting the end of the Camille affair, Berlioz stayed at Nice for a while and composed his *King Lear* overture. He had not seen the play, only read it, but the reading so affected him that it caused him, so he claimed, to roll in the grass in order to appease his uncontrollable enthusiasm.

Harriet, his first wife, had remained a remote Shakespearian vision for several years before they met — she was Ophelia or

Juliet and had become merged in his mind with De Quincy's opium dream and the *idée fixe* theme of the *Fantastic Symphony* before one spoken word had passed between them. He thus married an image and an ideal whom he only subsequently discovered to be a woman of flesh and private feelings. Marie Recio, the woman of his middle years — first as mistress then as second wife — seems not to have attracted any romantic passion, although others did from time to time. He always retained a need to love and be loved at an abnormal intensity, and experienced an abnormal loneliness of spirit when love was absent. The intensity and the loneliness may be judged from a reading of the passages in his *Memoirs* where he describes his journeys and finally successful attempts to meet Estelle Fornier. Highly dramatised, no doubt, but in places deeply moving. During his first search, in a mood of great sadness following his father's death in 1848, he pauses to reflect:

> Over there, where those young beech trees are shooting up, is where my father and I sat, and I played him 'Nina's Musette' on the flute. Estelle must have come here. Perhaps I stand in the very same portion of air where her enchanting form once stood. Now — look! I turn and take in the whole picture: the blessed house, its garden, its trees, below it the valley and the winding Isère and beyond, the Alps, the glaciers, the far-off gleaming snow — everything her eyes looked on. I breathe in the blue air that she breathed . . . . Ah! A cry re-echoes from the Saint-Eynard, a cry such as no human language can convey. Yes, I see, I see again, I behold, I worship. The past is before me, I am a boy of twelve. Life, beauty, first love, the infinite poetry of existence! I throw myself on my knees and cry, 'Estelle! Estelle!' to the valley and the hills and the sky. I clasp the earth in a convulsive embrace and bite the grass. And it begins: an access of loneliness, intense, overwhelming, indescribable. Bleed, my heart! Bleed! Only, leave me the power to suffer.[140]

This mood of tragic despair is reflected in the *Funeral March* for Hamlet, also produced in the shadow of his father's death and partly inspired by a London performance of the play seen in that eventful year of 1848. This same production, which sent him into ecstasies of praise for Shakespeare, caused him also to rearrange his sadly beautiful *Death of Ophelia* for female chorus and orchestra. Later, these two Shakespearean pieces joined the early *Religious Meditation*, based on Moore, to form the triptych *Tristia* (sadness). Despairing sadness is the stuff of suicide, a subject appearing as a minor thread at intervals in Berlioz's music to link Ophelia (above) with Dido, Cassandra and the Trojan woman in *The Trojans*, the two lovers in *Romeo and Juliet*, and Caesar's widow in *The Death of Cleopatra*. This last was a subject thrust upon the young composer in 1829 by his Prix de Rome examiners, but he linked it in his mind with Shakespeare and quoted Juliet at the head of the score: "How if, when I am laid in the tomb".

Paradoxically, sadness and a tomb-like loneliness were never far from the idea of love in Berlioz's mind. This link was perfected in 'Absence' — his favourite song from *Nuits d'Été* — and also in 'Sur les Lagunes' and 'Le Spectre de la Rose' from the same cycle, the latter echoing the fact that for him the scent of a beautiful rose evoked feelings of ideal romantic love. It was such a love that he attributed to the King of Thule in the moving ballad of that name in his *Faust*, and which, so he tells us near the end of his *Memoirs*, he felt for Estelle right at the end of his life — a passion of such power that not even Shakespeare could have imagined it. Only Thomas Moore, he says, believed in the possibility of such devotion, a devotion which inspired poignant letters to the elderly widow and that led him back to worship "the soft blue star that brightened the morning of my life".[141]

If Estelle symbolised love coupled with nature (he called her his *stella montis* — star of the mountains), Harriet did likewise with poetry. His passion for her "came to me with Shakespeare . . . . a voice out of the burning bush, among the lightning flashes and thunderclaps of a poetry that was new to me. It struck me down, my heart and whole being were possessed by a fierce, desperate passion in which love of the artist [Harriet] and of the art were interfused, each intensifying the other".[142]

Shakespeare remained forever a source of powerful inspiration for Berlioz. Following a successful performance of the *Romeo and Juliet* symphony at St. Petersburg in 1847, he again coupled this poetic obsession with the yearning for a perfect love, a "vision of a Juliet ever dreamed of, ever sought, never attained; of the revelation of unbounded love, infinite grief; and of . . . . joy that his [the composer's] music had caught a few far-off echoes of that starry poetry of the

spheres".[143] Love and music were frequently united in
Berlioz's mind, and indeed appear indissolubly linked on the
very last page of his *Memoirs*:

> Love or music — which power can uplift man to the sublimest
> heights? It is a large question; yet it seems to me that one should
> answer it in this way: Love cannot give an idea of music; music can
> give an idea of love. But why separate them? They are the two wings
> of the soul.[144]

But his faith incorporated a third wing, the uplifting power
of poetry, united with the others by an all-embracing sacra-
ment: worship of the divine creativity in man.

In his own art he venerated Gluck, Weber and Spontini, all
pioneers in expanding the dramatic expressiveness of music.
But he bowed down in awe before Beethoven, whose music,
even if performed only in the mind, could affect him "so that
little by little I fell into one of those unearthly ecstasies and
wept my eyes out at the sound of that tonal radiance which
only angels wear. Believe me . . . . the being who wrote such a
marvel of inspiration was not a man. Only thus does the
archangel Michael sing, as he dreamily contemplates the
spheres".[145]

Elsewhere he likens Beethoven — whom he always referred
to as a poet or a poet-musician, never a mere composer — to
an eagle who "hovers poised in his harmonious sky! He dives
into it, loses himself in it, soars, swoops again, disappears;
then returns to his starting-place, his eye more brilliant, his
pinions stronger, intolerant of rest, quivering, athirst for the
infinite![146] Such were Berlioz's feelings of empathy for
Beethoven that he could even modify his usual distrust of
public taste when this great poet was involved, sensing that
Beethoven's 'infinite' somehow managed to encompass the
common man:

> The public — that is to say the 'real' public, in the sense of that
> which does not belong to any coterie and which judges by senti-
> ment and not according to the narrow ideas and ridiculous theories
> which it has formed upon the subject of art — this public which, in
> spite of itself, makes mistakes, as is proved by the fact of its fre-
> quently having to alter its decisions, was, at the very onset, struck by
> some of the eminent qualities of Beethoven.[147]

If Beethoven was an archangel, then Shakespeare was God

himself. It was he who had first brought Berlioz face to face with Harriet in 1827, when the young composer found himself with a whole galaxy of exploding romantic talent — Hugo, Delacroix, de Vigny, Dumas, Nerval, Gautier — to be shaken by the Bard's turbulent poetry. Many years later, describing the grief and pity that welled over him when Harriet died, he appealed to the poet:

> Shakespeare! Shakespeare! I feel as if he alone of all men who ever lived can understand me, must have understood us both; he alone could have pitied us, poor unhappy artists, loving yet wounding each other. Shakespeare! You were a man. You, if you still exist, must be a refuge for the wretched. It is you that are our father, our father in heaven, if there is a heaven. God standing aloof in his infinite unconcern is revolting and absurd. Thou alone for the souls of artists art the living and loving God. Receive us, father, into thy bosom, guard us, save us! *De profundis ad te clamo.** What are death and nothingness? Genius is immortal![148]

This is clearly a piece of worship, and if the works of Shakespeare be regarded as some sort of bible, then Berlioz indeed practised a minor religion with its Holy City at Stratford-on-Avon. In his last years he indulged in readings from the master to gathered friends, an activity which he came to regard as an essential emotional hygiene, if not actually a piece of liturgy. It is interesting to note that in his divine capacity Shakespeare is a very personal, theistic God, far from the vague unfeeling force behind the universe to which He (it!) had been relegated by the 18th century deists. The latter had made it impossible for the rational Berlioz to believe in a supernatural heaven, but the romantic Berlioz wanted God to be a creative genius nevertheless — if there should happen to be a heaven after all.

Although very personal to Berlioz, the 'secular religion' of which Shakespeare formed a part was in some respects a symptom of the age in France, where a host of sects competed for the attention of those who could no longer accept a conventional heaven but who still felt the need for some sort of religious ideology. The choice was wide, ranging from theophilanthropy (a deistic survival from revolutionary times whose saints included Socrates, Rousseau and Washington),

*From the depths we cry to thee

via Saint-Simonism, to faith in evolution, progress (shades of
Condorcet from the previous century), the liberating power
of science, positivism (eventually incorporated into Comte's
'Church of Humanity'), Mesmer's 'animal magnetism',
spiritualism, Pierre Leroux's religious socialism, various
species of theosophy (Berlioz used Swedenborg's 'infernal
language' for the demons in *Faust*), many occult sects, and a
number of universal ('syncretist') religions. For those who
sought a middle way between superstitious and atheistic
extremes there was the popular eclecticism of Victor Cousin,
comprising a somewhat rationalistic 'natural religion' and
philosophy of history, the whole package derived from Plato
via Spinoza, Kant and Hegel, with sprinklings from the best
in all faiths and a belief in immortality without actually
affirming or denying the existence of a specific heaven.

But heaven or no heaven, Berlioz certainly knew his Shakespearean scriptures, if we are to judge by the number of
passages mentioned or quoted in his writings. Jacques Barzun
counted 150 such references, drawn from 21 of the 34
plays,[149] and it seems that the composer knew *Hamlet* by
heart in French, and eventually much of it in English − a
language which he made a determined effort to master over
the years, it being doubtful whether he understood very
much in 1827. His Shakespearean devotion is nicely underlined by the story of his attendance at the funeral of a friend,
told by Auguste Barbier. Berlioz showed absolutely no sign
of emotion, even as the coffin was lowered into the grave,
but when poet and composer were later taking tea together
and reading *Hamlet*, Berlioz was quite overcome by Shakespeare's tragedy and collapsed in tears. Barbier commented
that Art could softn this heart even when the most tragic
personal loss left him unmoved.

Virgil stirred him as a boy and Shakespeare as a man, the
one for heroic passions set in the stern mould of classical
tragedy, the other for a dramatic art so diversified as to
reflect all the depth, complexity, comedy, terror and beauty
of human existence − an 'open form' which profoundly
influenced his musical forms. The two converged in Berlioz's
mind to create *The Trojans*, the text of which he described
as 'Virgil Shakespeareanised'. This was partly because he had
shattered classical forms to accommodate a wide range of
emotional tones, and partly because the love duet of Dido

and Aeneas in the fourth act is actually an adaptation of the exchanges between Lorenzo and Jessica in the fifth act of *The Merchant of Venice*. The Princess Sayn-Wittgenstein, whose friendly persuasion and encouragement had spurred Berlioz to make a start on his masterpiece, wrote in praise of the libretto he had sent her for comment in 1856, to which he replied:

> it was not necessary to try and lure me on with eulogies that I do not deserve — it is beautiful because it is Virgil: it is striking because it is Shakespeare. I know it. I am only an interloper: I have ransacked the gardens of two geniuses, and cut a swathe of flowers to make a couch for music, where God grant she may not perish overcome by the fragrance.[150]

Three years later, when the characters and their feelings had been rendered in music and the task was complete, he declared that whatever fate may be in store for *The Trojans*, he now felt a companionable happiness: "I have spent my life with this race of demi-gods; I know them so well that I feel they must have known me".[151] He had come full circle: Dido's farewell, which had moved him to tears as a child, was now set in place at the end of a vast fresco designed to move others.

> Farewell, proud city, raised
> By selfless toil so swiftly to prosperity.
> My gentle sister, who shared my wanderings,
> Farewell. My people, farewell — and you, blessed shore
> Which welcomed me when I begged for refuge.
> Farewell fair skies of Africa, stars I gazed upon in wonder
> On those nights of boundless ecstasy and joy —
> I shall see you no more, my life comes to its end.

This could almost be Berlioz's own epitaph, uttered with gratitude for the brief joys of creation which precede oblivion. He certainly had many gloomy doubts about the ability of his music to survive — especially *The Trojans*, a work of epic but severe classical grandeur not to be taken seriously by a Paris opera audience nurtured on the ephemeral spectacles of Meyerbeer.

But music triumphant was truly part of Berlioz's artistic Godhead. It could, as he admitted, be merely a pleasant diversion for the mind . . . limit itself to tickling the ear. But when it concentrates at one and the same time all its powers on the sense of hearing . . . on the nervous system . . . the circulation . . . the brain which it sets on fire, the heart which it fills and quickens, the mind which it enlarges beyond measure and launches into the infinite, then it is acting in its proper realm . . . and I hardly know what other power it could seriously be compared with. Then it is that we are gods, and if men on whom fortune has heaped its favours could understand our ecstasies and buy them, they would squander their gold to share them for a moment.[152]

Berlioz so valued such elation and ecstasies, and so adored the artists whose works could produce them, that he was wont to engage in great outbursts of rage against adapters and meddlers, those who attacked what he called "the inalienable rights of the human spirit".[153] As noted previously, he even included such a tirade in one of his works for performance, *Lélio*, where the artist harangues the audience on the rights and wrongs of the creative life. In one sense his *Memoirs* are also conceived as such a lecture, a fully documented warning to all creative artists that they are alone in the universe and must not expect more than spasmodic assistance from an indifferent and often hostile world.

His private holy trinity of music, poetry and love was, for him, no rockbed of dogmatic certainty, but a precariously poised jewel needing an armed guard forever on the alert against a surrounding sea of mediocrity. Berlioz saw himself as one of the Knights of an artistic Holy Grail, a precious vessel moulded over the centuries by Virgil, Shakespeare, Beethoven — all the great creators — and which must be kept intact to provide vital energies for the imaginative spirit.

13

The Creative Imagination

Drawing together the threads of Berlioz's psyche — or rather, looking back for some pattern discernible in the tangled warp and woof of actuality — is there an essential Hector Berlioz? Have our twin apogees of Romantic and Rationalist encompassed the span of his spirit and intellect, or had he really several spirits and many intellects? Perhaps the interplay of personality and ideas, each influencing the other, will always make it impossible to isolate an ideology without distorting its meaning. Certainly the sharply glittering contrasts of Berlioz's personality are reflected in his ideas as clearly as in his music. Perhaps more so, for music cannot encompass the world of exact description amenable to words.

Similarities between the moods sensed in his music and expressed in his writings may be emphasized by juxtaposing the comments of two critics: Winton Dean on the music and David Cairns on the writing. Dean: "Here we approach the heart of Berlioz; a compound of energy, melancholy and serene detachment, an unfathomable sadness beneath a shimmering surface of high spirits".[154] Cairns: "The mixture of vivacity, wit, sadness, panache, dreamy exaltation, fierce partisanship, frankness, generous indignation and hauteur is characteristically Berliozian".[155] His contemporary and friend Ernest Legouvé, dramatist and poet, left some impressions of Berlioz the man which, again, could be held up as a mirror to reflect many aspects of both mind and music:

> Everything in Berlioz was original. An extraordinary mixture of enthusiasm and mockery; a mind that you could never predict;

conversation that had you constantly on the alert by its very change-
ability: long brooding silences, with lowered eyes and a glance that
seemed to plumb unimaginable depths — then a sudden dazzling
recovery of spirits, a stream of brilliant, amusing or touching remarks, bursts of Homeric laughter, and a delight like a child's.[156]

This was the clothing, the external mood, for a mind that was
creative musician, thinker, writer, lover, wit, poet, dreamer.
We know Berlioz primarily for his music, but few composers
illustrate more aptly Dr. Johnson's assertion (of the scholar/
poet/diplomat Abraham Cowley) that the "true genius is a
mind of large general powers, accidentally determined to
some particular direction".

Berlioz's direction was determined very largely by the contrast between his creative vision and the political practicalities of mid-19th century France. But while 'practicalities' of
one sort or another are a perennial obstacle to creative
innovation, his own acceptance of the challenge within a
particularly uncomprehending society invites us to see Berlioz
as an exemplar for all imaginative spirits. Colin Davis — an
interpreter of Berlioz the musician, not Berlioz the prophet —
draws upon Blake's vision of embattled categories to declare
that the composer's essence is in "the contrast between what
you can *imagine* and the satanic fact, which is why he will
always be contemporary".[157] A parallel comment on the
continuing relevance of his vision comes from David Cairns:
"Berlioz is an artist that we can especially respond to today:
a clear-sighted, unsentimental humanist, a stoic whose vision
of grandeur is free of illusions, a poet whose profound sense
of beauty does not close his eyes to chaos lurking at the edge
of civilisation".[158]

That lurking chaos, together with the withering psychological disease of isolation, drove him at times to despair.
Yet, in the manner of Legouvé's character sketch, sudden
shafts of creative light could scatter the gloom, or coexist
with it in some strange counterpoint of the mind. Thus in
the two years between the deaths of his sister Adèle and his
second wife, Marie, following unsuccessful attempts to get
his beloved *Trojans* accepted by the Paris Opéra, he composed *Beatrice and Benedict*, a nimble miracle of lightness,
tenderness and enchanting humour based on Shakespeare's
Much Ado About Nothing — albeit with the addition of an

unsavoury musical pedant called Somarone, a caricature for Berlioz and his audience to laugh at. At this very time he wrote:

> I am in my sixty-first year, past hopes, past illusions, past high thoughts and lofty conceptions. My son is almost always far away from me. I am alone. My contempt for the folly and baseness of mankind, my hatred of its atrocious cruelty, have never been so intense. And I say hourly to Death: 'When you will'. Why does he delay? [159]

How genuine was this contempt for humanity, even in the bitter last years? Saint-Saëns said that he "depicted himself in his *Memoirs* in very false colours, pretending to hate mankind, he who the smallest mark of sympathy moved to tears. He only hated the *profanum vulgus*,* like Horace, like all artists and all poets".[160] It is interesting to note that Beethoven, a puritanical bachelor who loved his mother dearly but thought little of his father, was rude and difficult in many of his personal relationships yet often declared his love of humanity; Berlioz, a sexual libertarian, felt deep affection for his father and apparently little for his mother, was sociable, friendly, paid his moral and financial debts, yet frequently declared his hatred of mankind. But these opposite types who shared a raging belief in the redeeming power of music were also united in a very personal matter: Beethoven's notoriously overbearing attitude to his surrogate son, the adopted nephew Karl, was echoed in Berlioz's inflexible treatment of his own son Louis. Indeed, it has been suggested that as a father the Frenchman is seen in his least humane rôle.[161]

But such thoughts are best left to followers of Freud, who may scorn this book's acceptance of conscious beliefs and feelings as viable materials in their own right. Likewise, some Marxists will find diverse economic factors to explain Berlioz without listening to what he has to say. However, while it has seemed reasonable to the author to pursue one particular mystery into unconscious realms (see Appendix), to open the floodgates of psychoanalysis or of wealth and social class would be to sidestep the rationale of this study, which for better or worse employs the existential facts of thought

*common people

and feeling as its material.

Summarising the ideological pattern traced by that material, it could be said that Berlioz's youthful idealism — the expectation of a society renewed by art and science — was gradually eroded by the nagging gap between imagination and social fact, to be replaced by a very personal devotion to his own creative art. But while he could worship nature, music and poetry with true feeling in the manner of his fellow Romantics, and even at times experience religious emotions, he remained agnostic in the matter of religious belief and expected no heaven beyond that attained fleetingly, by a few, in this world.

His disillusion with politics and a growing distrust of democracy were due partly to the philistine commercialism with which they were associated in his mind, although sometimes this association weakened and sparks of radical indignation shone through from his youth. Despite an early sympathy with national struggles against the Austrian Empire, his allegiance to Enlightenment universalism eventually merged with a lingering Saint-Simonian internationalism to create an intense dislike of national patriotism. In this he was against the trend of the century, which at first coupled emergent nationalism with democracy in the idealistic manner of the Italian propagandist Mazzini (an amalgam which Berlioz soon came to distrust), and later turned to the political and military 'realism' by which Cavour and Bismarck created nation-states by balancing power and wielding force (which Berlioz detested). With his pacifist hatred of violence and generally humanitarian views on the smaller social questions, this would make him — in modern terms — an aristocratic, sceptical, artistically idealistic, but rather stoically disenchanted liberal.

In addition to the example he may set as a defender of art against barbarism, Berlioz typifies the whole range of competing attitudes which our century inherits from the key minds of its two predecessors. The 18th century, Age of Enlightenment and the Encyclopaedists, refined the doctrines of rational order and produced the hope that man could improve his lot simply by abandoning past superstitions and social structures and adopting the life of Reason. The refinement and the hope were partly shattered by the French Revolution but have remained at the root of the reasoned liberalism of later generations.

The 19th century, the Romantic Age, turned against this oversimplified view of the world and searched rather for deeper meanings. It respected feelings and the transforming power of imagination as at least the equal of analytical reasoning, and particularly honoured individual creative insight. It also looked to the past to gain an organic view of history and our ritual function within it. Art, religion and spiritual things in general were elevated — especially music, which the theologian Freidrich Schleiermacher referred to as "a special self-contained revelation of the world".[162]

If positivist philosophy, mechanistic science and literary or artistic 'realism' seemed to be working in the reverse sense towards the end of Berlioz's life, there were eventually romantic reactions: the emergence of Symbolism in French literature for instance. Likewise, the conviction that man and the universe are more complex and less predictable than a naïve 'scientism' would have us believe has re-emerged in our own time, and may be seen as a romantic response to a materialistic rationalism. The rational and romantic spirits are in us all, the one mixed up with 'classical' because part of the romantic revolt was against a particular aesthetic convention rather than against reason as such, the other easily condemned as 'licence' because of our laziness in recognising patterns requiring the abandonment of comfortable preconceptions. Confused or not, the two outlooks may be seen at work, competing and balancing on an unstable see-saw in every corner of modern existence.

We cultivate our straight and well-ordered flowerbeds but long for wild mountain scenery. We assume that public money should be spent on entertainment to satisfy the widest audience, yet feel that society should subsidise concerts and operas for the sake of 'Art'. A rational plan to build a car-park can be thwarted by romantically rooted legislation which prevents destruction of a ruined castle on the proposed site. Educationists are divided between advocates of a Rousseau-like freedom for children at school, in the romantic belief that this encourages individual creativity, and those who enforce an atmosphere of rational order.Time-honoured and romantically colourful ceremonies continue unchanged — and almost unchallenged — despite their admitted irrelevance on a purely rational plane. And so on. But whether a person is essentially rational or romantic, he will usually regard himself as 'reasonable': a universal label for behaviour which fits current social attitudes. Berlioz was fully attuned to this when he said that the 'reasonable people' who support arranged marriages should be stuffed into a sack with 100,000 pounds of good sense and thrown into the sea.

Oversimplifying to make a point: 18th century man believed that taste in poetry is no more important than taste in women's clothes, and that impartial truth, order and equality are supreme virtues; 19th century man believed that Art and the creative ego are of transcendental importance, and that myth, variety and greatness should be our guides. In a torn and erratic manner, modern man manages to subscribe to both philosophies. This is what Berlioz did, out of his time, which makes him our contemporary in an even fuller sense than Colin Davis intended.

Berlioz, remember, was the rational humanitarian who objected to the throat-slitting of a shrove-tide bull, but was also the romantic elitist who protested against paying taxes on concert receipts. He condemned the irrational notion that music could depict landscape, yet enthused romantically that Beethoven had done this very thing so well. The sceptic in him scorned the claims of table-turning Spiritualists, but the believer went into ecstasies over mystical feelings inspired by *The Infant Christ.* He dismissed the absurdity of creating work for work's sake in 1848, but supported free musical education for children. He may have been odd in his own time, but we see him everywhere today.

Above all, Hector Berlioz was a visionary champion of the creative urge in man, an intense believer in the fragile concept of beauty and in our capacity and duty to seek the beautiful against all odds. He once declared that his whole life had been one ardent pursuit of an ideal formed in his own imagination. It is our good fortune that through the constructive power of that imagination his ideal world has been enshrined in music — in an art where beauty is moulded with the elegance and passion so characteristic of his mind.

Appendix

THE EMMET CONNECTION

There is a history in all men's lives,
Figuring the nature of the times deceas'd.
                                    Shakespeare.

This appendix pursues the curious matter of Berlioz's links with the Irish revolutionary patriot Robert Emmet. Various oddities in the composer's life and attitudes pointing to some deep connection were touched on briefly in Chapter 7, but further speculations at that point would have involved a lengthy digression from the book's main theme, so the relevant material has been assembled here for separate assessment. It is presumed that the reader has studied the complete book, but absorption of Chapter 7 in particular is necessary before tackling the following pages.

It will be useful to set the scene with a potted biography of Emmet, culled from several complete studies of the Irishman.[163] Beyond this, relevant facts have been distilled from the available sources wherever there seem to be patterns of Berliozian significance.

●   ●   ●

Robert Emmet was the youngest son in a nominally Protestant but deistically inclined and politically liberal upper middle-class Irish family. His father was a doctor of medicine with classical interests and literary leanings. His brother Thomas Addis Emmet was involved in the 1798 uprising against British rule and eventually settled in the U.S. to become an honoured man of the law at the American bar. He died in November 1827 at just about the time Berlioz claimed to have been overwhelmed by Moore's poem about the younger Emmet.

Robert, a rather grave boy, was clever at chemistry, fond of music, and had an early talent for drawing and modelling which led him to become no mean amateur at relief sculpture. He was noted as a brilliant and sincere speaker of radical and democratic sympathies while he was a student with Thomas Moore at Trinity College Dublin. On one occasion, during a College debate on whether a soldier should always obey orders, he argued that humanity must come first and that disobedience could be justified — rather as Berlioz was to feel about the Austro-Prussian war seventy years later. Of Robert's personal character, Moore always retained an indelible impression of gentle uprightness to complement his political and ethical ideals.

Studies were cut short when Emmet left Trinity College during a political purge after the 1798 revolt, and in 1800/1802 he travelled in Europe, where he worked with other Irish exiles on schemes to involve France as an ally against British rule — in the manner of 1798, when France had landed a small force in Ireland to support the rebellion. The following lines by Emmet probably refer to this period:

> Far from my country I am driven,
> A wanderer sent from thee;
> But still my constant prayer to heaven
> Shall be to make thee free. [164]

While Emmet and his friends had no illusions concerning France's illiberal ruthlessness under Napoleon and had every intention of resisting the French as well as the British if necessary, they tried to persuade Bonaparte and his Foreign Minister Talleyrand to co-operate again with the optimistic but by then much weakened United Irish Movement. It was suggested that the French should time an invasion of England to coincide with an uprising in Ireland. There was indeed a considerable gathering of forces in Northern France, with a great encampment at Boulogne which, by the Spring of 1803,

Britain regarded as a breach of the peace signed at the Treaty of Amiens. A smaller French force gathered at Brest for transport to Ireland, but Emmet sensed little more than token support and returned to Dublin in the Autumn of 1802, where he went ahead with plans for a revolt which matured in the following July. The plot failed and after a short period on the run Emmet, aged 25, was captured, put on trial for treason and hanged, leaving the unhappy Sarah Curran to face her father's anger and the world's pity.

A sense of pity inspired a number of commemorations, notably Washington Irving's 'The Broken Heart', based on Sarah's story and included in his *Sketch Book*, and Moore's poem 'She is far from the land where her young hero sleeps' — written after her death in 1808 and included in the volume of translations from which Berlioz extracted 'Élégie'. Robert Southey wrote some verses in tribute to Emmet in 1803, and Shelley composed some lines after visiting his unengraved tomb in 1812. Prose commentaries are legion, and the neo-Protestant Robert Emmet who said 'let no man write my epitaph' is now an established folk hero of Catholic Ireland. Thomas Moore honoured the letter if not the spirit of Emmet's plea for silence with some lines beginning:

> Oh! breathe not his name, let it sleep in the shade
> Where cold and unhonoured his relics are laid.

Moore remained loyal to the memory of Emmet and has probably been the greatest single influence in the survival of his name. Thirty-five years after Emmet's death on the gallows in Dublin, Moore dined with the Irish Chief Secretary in Dublin Castle and made a point of praising the young man who had dared to challenge British rule by attempting to storm that very building. Moore recorded this incident in his *Journal* in a manner conveying thankfulness and pride that he had attempted such a daring act of vindication. It was probably around this very time (Autumn 1838, when the singer Alizard was preparing some concerts with the composer) that Berlioz finally decided not to alter his 'Élégie' but to leave it simply as a song for piano and solo voice. It was almost as if he were aware of the poet's proud Dublin gesture and of the fact that Moore and Emmet had once shared the simple pleasure of singing at the piano, hence his feeling that it would indeed be 'a kind of sacrilege' if his own spontaneous tribute were tampered with.

On one of those youthful occasions when Emmet and Moore were at the piano going through old Gaelic songs while they chatted about their country's plight, Moore played the air known as 'The Red Fox', the melody used as a setting for his poem 'Let Erin remember the days of old'. Moore describes the episode in his *Memoirs* as follows: "He used frequently to sit by me at the pianoforte, while I played over the airs . . . . and I remember one day when we were thus employed, his starting up, as if from a reverie, while I was playing the spirited air 'Let Erin remember the Days', and exclaiming passionately: 'Oh! that I were at the head of twenty thousand men marching to that air'."

This seems to envisage a revolutionary situation, although Emmet's eventual revolt was a fairly stealthy affair and he certainly didn't use any music when leading the Dublin rebellion in July 1803. Berlioz, also a 'July revolutionary' happened to enact a little of Emmet's vision on the occasion in 1830 when he led a crowd singing the *Marseillaise*, a grandly Gallic episode which grew from a curiously Celtic beginning. Berlioz relates how, to his astonished delight, he discovered "that a dozen or so young men were engaged in singing a battle hymn of my composition, the words of which, translated from Moore's *Irish Melodies*, happened to suit the situation exactly".[165] The song was 'Chant Guerrier' (War Song) from *Neuf Mélodies* published a few months earlier, based on two of Moore's more extravertly patriotic pieces and forming the third song in the cycle which culminates with 'Élégie'. Despite its heroic subject, 'Chant Guerrier' is an improbably sophisticated piece to be sung spontaneously in the open air by a crowd of youngsters. Or was the spirit of Robert Emmet perhaps lurking in the vicinity, observing this rather more successful revolution and exerting some occult influence to favour Moore and Berlioz?

Stretching the imagination further, one might see an alternative partial fulfilment of Emmet's marching dream in 1840, when Berlioz led massed instrumentalists of the National Guard in an open-air performance of the *Funeral and Triumphal Symphony*, a large part of which involved a slow march. The composer wore a military uniform for the event, and while various stories that he either dreamed of conducting with a sword, or actually did so, are difficult to confirm, the affair does suggest a parallel with Emmet's somewhat flamboyant donning of a green and gilt uniform with sword during the final hours of his abortive revolt.

It happens that the vigorous choral finale added by Berlioz for concert performances of the symphony uses words about liberty and the heroic dead which are very much in the spirit of Emmet's own jottings on the same subject. Also, the composer himself seems to have been rather more carried away by the ethos of the work than would be expected from his political attitudes ten years after the July revolution; or even later, when he still wrote enthusiastically on the subject in his *Memoirs*. As noted in Chapter 5, the 1840 occasion was a re-interment of the July heroes beneath a column erected on the site of the Bastille, an honour whose equivalent was denied to countless United Irishmen cast into a common grave behind the Royal Barracks in Dublin and celebrated by Emmet in some verses beginning:

> No rising column marks this spot,
> Where many a victim lies,
> But, oh, the blood which here has streamed
> To heaven for justice cries.[166]

Whether or not the winged figure of Liberty on a 'rising column' erected in Paris provided some curious fulfilment of Emmet's plea for justice made in Dublin forty years before, it occurred to the author that there might be a more musical factor to link Emmet's enthusiasm for 'Let Erin remember' with Berlioz's enthusiasm for 'When he who adores thee' — perhaps something about the respective melodies, heard by one and created by the other. Careful examination shows that there is in fact a close thematic resemblance between the opening phrase of 'Élégie' and that of the Red Fox tune. While this brief similarity may have little objective significance, it prompted the thought that Berlioz might have been thrust into his 1827 spasm of creativity by the *joint* impact of 'Let Erin remember' and 'When he who adores thee', an hypothesis requiring that he discovered the two items simultaneously. Investigation revealed that the translations were indeed immediately adjacent in the collection used by Berlioz, and one wonders whether the unique coalescence of emotional impulse and creative act reported by the composer in response to 'When he who adores thee' was in some mysterious fashion an echo of Emmet's uniquely enthusiastic reaction to 'Let Erin remember' printed on the preceding page. At some level, somewhere, those verses about Erin implied a tune, and if some of that tune found its way into 'Élégie', might this have been because of an imperative unconscious force dictating a brief musical parody from the past? A sort of *Karma* with the cause in one life and the effect in another? But whether or not cause and effect may be detached in this way across time, there are some rather more personal resemblances of character between Berlioz and Emmet to add to the list of coincidences. Consider the following three comments:

> . . . . a pale, tense young man, with regular features, slim figure and commanding air. One could hardly fail to notice such a strikingly forceful face, with its fine sardonic smile, eyes deep-set and alternately full of fire and veiled with melancholy, faithfully reflecting the play of his passionate, mercurial feelings.[167]

> His face is uncommonly expressive of everything youthful, and everything enthusiastic, and his colour comes and goes so rapidly, accompanied by such a nervousness of agitated sensibility, that in his society I feel in a perpetual apprehension . . . his reserve prevents one's hearing many of his opinions, yet one would swear to their style of exaltation, from their flitting shadows blushing across his countenance in everlasting succession.[168]

> [He] exhibited rare and brilliant faculties, a singular blending of enthusiasm and sagacity, a great power of concentration, an ardent and poetical fancy, combined with an exact and penetrating intellect.[169]

Two of these described Robert Emmet and one refers to the young Hector Berlioz, but could any reader who had not previously seen these texts say which is which? Is the ardent poetry and penetrating intellect in the third piece an aspect of Berlioz the rational romantic or Emmet the artistic revolutionary? Does the mercurial interplay of fire and melancholy in the first quotation apply to Berlioz or Emmet, and does it paraphrase the flitting shadows of sensibility mentioned in the second?

In fact the first comment is on Berlioz by the music publisher Léon Escudier, the second on Emmet as seen in Paris by Catherine Wilmot (a lady doing the 'grand tour' in

1801) and the third also on Emmet by Mme. de Staël's grand-daughter the Comtesse d'Haussonville. Consider also Legouvé's description of Berlioz quoted on page 107. This concerned the mature man, but allow for the greater diffidence of youth and compare this with the above impressions of Emmet. It could be the same person.

Returning to Mme. de Staël, Emmet used to visit the famous lady's salon in Paris and made a favourable impression which was passed on as family gossip, eventually prompting her grand-daughter to write a book on the Irishman.* Of the social life to be had in Paris around 1800, that in the salon of Mme. de Staël was probably the least frivolous, most Germanically high-minded and critically radical — hence the good lady's periodic exile by Napoleon, who couldn't abide her Protestant liberalism and her allegiance to Montesquieu's doctrine of the separation of powers. It seems from what we know of Emmet (whose father, it appears, had also met this influential woman) that he disliked the polished but empty chatter common in French society and thus gravitated naturally to this haven of intellect and art. Shades of Berlioz! The composer would always choose an earnest discussion about poetry, music or philosophy in preference to exchanges about dress or social niceties.

But a 'shade' is really a ghost, and Berlioz was not yet born when Emmet made his impressions in France. If there are any shades in this story they are those of Emmet in the life of Berlioz, and our problem is to decide if the apparent links between the two men are simply patterns of chance, or whether the intersection of so many coincidences is evidence of a real but unconscious influence of one man upon the other.

The list is not yet complete, for Berlioz shared another passion with Emmet: the harp, which they both regarded as a supremely expressive instrument. Such an allegiance would be natural for Emmet, as the instrument is Ireland's national symbol and he loved the traditional music of his country, much of which employed the harp. His girl Sarah, who was very musical and rated Mozart well above Cimarosa, sang beautifully to her own harp accompaniment; he wrote a poem involving the harp ('Genius of Erin, tune thy harp');

Robert Emmet by Comtesse d'Haussonville, Paris 1858.

and he even designed and produced the seal of office of the United Irishmen, featuring a decorated harp of the traditional type in which a mermaid forms the column.

An ancient legend about the harp concerns this siren, whose golden hair is stretched to form the strings and whose tale Moore related in his poem 'The origin of the harp'. Berlioz used these verses for the seventh piece in *Irlande*, while in one published version of the songs an illustration on the cover combines the themes of musical and heroic Ireland in the figure of a defiant woman with one hand on a harp and the other on a sword. Emmet's seal depicted a woman playing the harp, but armed with axes and spears! Berlioz's own use of the harp and his large ambitions for the instrument were discussed in Chapter 8, but the strength of his personal attachment may be judged from a statement that if he were rich he would include two or three Erard harps among the instruments in his workroom. He even contrived to *live* in the Rue de la Harpe at about the time of the 'Élégie' episode.

Another slight coincidence is that both men had medical fathers, and although Dr. Emmet was fully trained while Dr. Berlioz was partly self-taught, each submitted a specialist thesis to medical authorities in Montpellier — both of which were subsequently published in Paris — and each was an Enlightenment man with wide literary interests. Also, French was the language normally spoken in both homes despite Emmet's Irish upbringing, while Latin equalled English as the second tongue in the Dublin household. Each of the latter languages finally became important enough in Berlioz's life for the composer to regard himself as an authority on the pronunciation of one and make a prolonged effort to learn the other. The Frenchman's and Irishman's handwritings also had a degree of family resemblance.

The penumbra of events surrounding Emmet and Ireland even managed to be particularly active in France during Berlioz's first full day on earth. On that day (12th December 1803) the French military authorities published a detailed scheme of command for the organisation of 30,000 to 40,000 men in the embarkation camp at Brest, scheduled as part of a plan for an invasion of Ireland. Although the invasion never took place, preparations were fairly extensive and would have matched the United Irishmen's hopes earlier in the year. But after the failure of Emmet's uprising the Movement's exiled leaders in Paris (including Robert's brother Thomas Addis) had little faith that anything would happen. However, one of Robert's last activities before his arrest was to send an emissary to Paris to urge an acceleration of the invasion now that Irish discontent had been demonstrated, and one could imagine his spirit hovering in whatever discarnate existence there may be, dreaming still of freedom for his country and gravitating hopefully to France as the military plans matured some three months after his execution. It could have seemed that Napoleon's ambitions might still provide an occasion for Ireland's detachment from Britain.

More specifically, as the infant Berlioz yelled for his first morning feed on that day of the published plan, the nearest military garrison (at Grenoble) was the one place in the whole of France from which a company of soldiers set forth as part of the accumulation of troops intended for Ireland.

The list of curiosities grows, but while a conjunction of two or three coincidences might reasonably be dismissed as the workings of chance, the total of such oddities is surely now too large for such a casual explanation. The curious mixture of attitudes *within* Berlioz, parallels *between* Berlioz and Emmet, and apparent interconnections of circumstance acting *beyond* them — all this comprises a jig-saw puzzle which interlocks so well across the boundaries of time and space that we need a less specious rational than mere 'coincidence', the sponge commonly employed to soak up inconvenient facts with an occult flavour.

The notion of ghostly influences has already been mooted, but if anything remotely psychical is to be considered it will be best if some of the options are listed more formally so that the reader may take his pick as the fancy strikes him in the admittedly somewhat fanciful pages to follow. Here is one possible list:

(1) That all the apparent connections are due to chance coincidences.

(2) That Berlioz read or was told the Emmet story when young, was greatly struck by it and identified himself with the Irish hero, but then totally forgot the tale and 'discovered' it again at a purely emotional level when he composed 'Élégie'. A sort of barely conscious cryptomnesia.

(3) That one man can somehow unconsciously influence another directly *across time* in such a manner as to mould

his attitudes and actions, and on occasion produce intense emotion.

(4) That a meaningful pattern of coincidences operating according to Jung's principle of synchronicity can apply not only across space (Moore and Berlioz in 1838?), but between people living at different times.

(5) That Berlioz was recurrently 'possessed' by Emmet's spirit to produce the same effects as in No. 3.

(6) That the composer was the recipient of multiple unconscious telepathic and clairvoyant impressions about the Irishman from minds and objects scattered around the world in his own time. A sort of super-ESP effect.

(7) That Hector Berlioz was a reincarnation of Emmet.

It may be thought that the complexities of the case require a mixture of several of these, although the last option will probably be regarded as the least credible by most Western readers. However, reincarnation is a common enough notion in many cultures and there are some cases where a considerable body of evidence remains stubbornly inexplicable on any other hypothesis, despite meticulous appraisal in a scientific spirit.[170] While the Berlioz/Emmet link is certainly not such a case, some form of metempsychosis would tie together and rationalise most of the jig-saw rather well, just as the superficially extreme idea of continental drift can now explain the jig-saw 'fit' of land masses on a not-so-solid earth. At least the conjecture is worth pursuing, however tentatively.

The proposal is that a ripple of the Irishman's psyche entered the embryonic composer some time between Emmet's death and Berlioz's birth 82 days later, to well up from the unconscious — unrecognised but powerfully felt — at crucial moments in his life. Reincarnation is conceived here as a layered mental existence in which one mind enwraps a set of traces taken in from an earlier mind, the 'outer' layer of contemporary consciousness being inclined to swamp the earlier traces as it grows into a firm personality in reaction to its present environment. Memories of previous existences (if indeed there are such) are thus extremely elusive and normally confined to childhood years, after which they tend to become forgotten or overlaid.

There is also the possibility that such traces may remain forever beneath consciousness, or perhaps be so tenuous that they provoke conscious reactions only in the form of vague feelings rather than as specific memories — the *déjà vu* effect. Professor Ian Stevenson, the leading Western authority on reincarnation, has pointed out that in the case of such very dim recollections of a previous life "the dormancy or arousal of these memories may depend upon whether or not these persons happen to come into contact with persons or places which provide the stimulation necessary to bring the memories above the threshold of consciousness."[171]

The suggestion here is that such memories were normally below the threshold for Berlioz, where they still nevertheless dictated some aspects of behaviour or attitude, but that on one very special occasion he became blindingly aware of a deep and mysterious personal involvement with the message contained in Moore's poem 'When he who adores thee'. It is notable that in describing the period of dazed wanderings during which he came across those verses Berlioz said that he 'looked like a man searching for his soul', while it may be significant that the event provoking this search was centred on an Irish girl (Harriet Smithson). If Berlioz's mind did incorporate something from Emmet's, one might expect a special reaction when he saw and heard a girl from Ireland who, to judge by the one authentic portrait we have of Sarah Curran,* was of the same facial type as Emmet's girl — at least to the extent of possessing a cherubic mouth, long gently curving nose and large expressive eyes. Also, Berlioz saw Harriet playing Ophelia and Juliet, whose mild sweet manner would fit the few extant descriptions of Sarah's personality. It would be intriguing to discover if anyone who had known Sarah Curran saw Harriet Smithson on the stage at a later date (she had appeared in several of the larger Irish towns within a dozen years of Sarah's death), and whether any resemblance was noted.

If, as Berlioz claimed, he already seemed to be 'searching for his soul' when he found Moore's poem, it could be that Harriet was the real trigger in this whole affair, not just the accidental creator of an infatuated and receptive state of mind. Did an unrecognized but emotionally compelling vision of Sarah set him adrift on an uncharted psychic sea,

*By Edward Corballis, 1802.

with Moore's lines about Emmet providing a further tantaliz-
ing glimpse of the past which acted as a catalyst to provoke
an explosion of creative self-discovery? Berlioz added the
inscription 'F.H.S.' to the first version of the song, popularly
supposed to mean 'for Harriet Smithson' — a natural enough
dedication for someone in love, but a further small link in the
chain of Irish circumstance. Remember, incidentally, that
Emmet's ex-revolutionary brother Thomas Addis died at just
about this time, and if we are provisionally accepting the
notion of transmigrating souls it could be that he also was
tugging at a buried layer (the Emmet layer?) of Berlioz's
mind.

If any of this rather abandoned speculation is acceptable
it raises the question of why, with many thousands of
babies waiting in wombs, Robert Emmet's Irish spirit should
turn up in Hector Berlioz's French body. This is part of a
general question about possible choice of subject if and when
spirits transmigrate. While most reincarnationist doctrines
accept a time gap between death and rebirth, views on how
or why a spirit goes to a particular body vary from an assump-
tion that it just happens automatically (destination unknown), via the traditional Buddhist doctrine of a succession
of rebirths at higher or lower levels, to belief in a simple
conscious choice. If the last applies, why should the Irishman
have chosen an embryo in the village of La Côte Saint-André
in a remote corner of France?

Those troops apparently destined for Ireland and about to
depart from nearby Grenoble may have had something to do
with it: a vague wisp of Irish awareness might have chosen to
slip in because of a vaguely Irish activity in the vicinity.
Alternatively (or in addition) Emmet may have formed a
prior attachment to the area at the suggestion of his father,
who had travelled extensively in France and knew some
regions very well. In his old age, Emmet senior had a private
game in which he would imagine himself as a student again,
choose a French river and name all the villages, bridges and
churches along its banks, as if travelling in a boat. Some of
this love of France probably affected his son, and it is even
possible that during his European travels Robert Emmet
visited places suggested by his father — perhaps looked up
old friends from Dr. Emmet's days at the University of
Montpellier. In any event, Emmet junior did travel from

Switzerland to the South of France in 1800, and the routes available at that time would have taken him via Lyons, or possibly even through Grenoble. Thus he saw some of the country into which Berlioz was to be born three years later and might even have decided that it was an ideal spot to which to return — albeit consciously as Emmet, not unconsciously as Berlioz.

But chosen or not, Emmet's reincarnation would not only link together the various Irish strands in Berlioz's life, but might also make more sense of some other aspects of the composer. One Berlioz oddity is that although he tended to be a hoarder of letters, he kept not a single one from his first wife Harriet. Her inadequate French and a frequently difficult and finally shattered relationship could be invoked to explain this, but it is still rather odd when one considers the large correspondence he did keep. Emmet's great 'fault', it will be recalled, was his failure to destroy incriminating letters from Sarah Curran, and if Harriet was indeed a sort of substitute for Sarah at some level of Berlioz's psyche, it could be that he felt guiltily compelled to destroy her letters.

He also sometimes felt an introspective compulsion bordering on the psychotic, suggestive of a mind divided from itself and searching for some lost but disturbing mystery. In February 1830, at a time when a revived and overwhelming passion for the Irish Harriet was driving him to distraction and towards composition of the *Fantastic Symphony*, and when he happened also to be working on the Thomas Moore Irish settings as he gathered together and finished the *Neuf Mélodies*, he wrote to his father about his state of mind:

> The habit of continual self-observation that I have acquired means that no sensation ever escapes me, and invariably I see myself in a mirror. I often experience extraordinary things which I find quite impossible to describe to you. My constant nervous excitement is the most likely cause of these hallucinations, which are comparable to those produced by opium-smoking. But what surprises me in particular is that I remember having had the same sort of experience when I was twelve: my memory re-lives those agonizing days which I went through in a state of unending agitation that had neither motive nor object.[172]

Was it really Berlioz he saw in a mirror during his hallucinations, or were the 'extraordinary things' which he found it impossible to describe actually glimpses of Emmet? At a less disturbing but still somewhat compulsive level were his words about the evening breeze over the lakes of Killarney, his search in London for the subject of Moore's lines, and his subsequent bi-lingual printing of highlights from Emmet's speech. Were these also examples of 'self-observation'? If the visions he had at the age of 26 were very similar to those experienced when he was twelve, it would certainly seem that some of the most powerful forces at work in his mind were established too early for explanation in terms of an adult imagination reacting to direct experiences.

It was at the age of twelve, remember, that he fell in love with Estelle Duboeuf, and a striking aspect of the infatuation is that Berlioz's strongest single memory of the girl was that she wore a pair of pink half-boots. Perhaps such footwear was rare in rural France in 1815, but it certainly appeared in England around 1800, and as Dublin fashions usually followed close behind those in London it could be that some Irish girls — perhaps even Sarah Curran herself — wore pink half-boots when Robert Emmet was dreaming of love as well as freedom. Was Estelle, Berlioz's first great passion, the victim of a mistaken identity because of her boots?

On a more serious level, his deep dislike of Protestantism is curious for a Frenchman whose reliance on a personal ethic was Protestant in spirit and who was in rational revolt against Catholic dogma, yet anyone fighting for Irish freedom (even a Protestant) would be very much aware of Puritan intolerance lurking in the background. It was this very intolerance that Berlioz chose to see as typical of the reformed churches in general, and which caused him actually to express a *preference* for Catholicism despite his disagreement with its doctrines — and despite a tradition of alliances between liberal Protestants and renegade Catholics. Such a deeply anti-Protestant attitude was much more likely in an Irishman, despite a widespread French awareness of Ireland's religious problems. It is also consonant with the deist Robert Emmet befriending the Catholic Thomas Moore and fighting for a mainly Catholic Ireland against an England whose presence had so often been equated with Cromwellian brutality.

The self-inflincted brutality of a suicidal funeral pyre brought on a show of intense 'Virgilian grief' in the young

Berlioz when he first read of Dido's death in the *Aeneid* —
again at around the age of twelve, during the days of 'un-
ending agitation'. It was not the death alone, perhaps, which
so affected him, but the whole situation of Aeneas' departure
and Dido's mad grief — her incapacity to understand that
love could be over-ruled by an ideological dream. Aeneas
sailed away because he was obsessed by a political destiny —
to found the Roman race — just as Emmet left his girl (or
was taken) because of a similar obsession with duty: to free
the Irish people. Was Berlioz's very unchildlike childhood
misery a small echo of the Emmet story, a reaction to a
pattern recognised at some level within his own experience?
If so, could it be that when his early grief was eventually
transmuted into great art in the final scene of *The Trojans*,
Berlioz's generous use of the harp drew unconsciously upon
Irish symbolism? At the supreme climax of the tragedy, as
Aeneas goes and Dido dies, he employed *six* harps to express
the inexpressible grandeur and grief of the moment.

A juxtaposition of harps and ancient mythology brings us
to the last and perhaps most fanciful of all these speculations.
It will be recalled from Chapter 8 that Berlioz especially
valued the adagio from his early competition cantata *The
Death of Orpheus*, which he later absorbed into *Lélio* and
which he found emotionally shattering in performance. The
story of Orpheus and Eurydice fascinated Berlioz right
through his life; he so loved Gluck's *Orphée*, for instance,
that he eventually prepared his own performing version in
1859. This strong attachment, coupled with his intense
feelings about the music he had composed to represent the
story's sad ending, suggests that there might be hidden here
another fragment of the Emmet saga, again symbolically disguised as a myth in Jungian style. Orpheus descended into
the underworld to rescue his loved-one, almost succeeded but
then met eventual catastrophe, Eurydice returning to perdi-
tion and Orpheus meeting death at the hands of the Bacchan-
tes — with Eurydice's name on his lips. Emmet descended
into the revoltuionary underworld to rescue Ireland, seemed
to be succeeding but then met disaster, his beloved country
remaining captive and himself meeting death from the British
— with Ireland's name on his lips.

Berlioz symbolised Orpheus' indestructible love for Eurydice with some lines of Thomas Moore quoted as a motto on

his cantata:

> The sunflower turns on her god, when he sets,
> The same look which she turned when he rose*.

It was the dejection and sorrow of the *aftermath* which Berlioz found particularly poignant in the Orpheus story, especially the harp now almost silent but once played so magnificently, and depicted so strikingly in his music of 1827 — just as he responded later in the same year to Moore's sad tale of Emmet's imagined aftermath. He was so concerned about the exact meaning of the *Orpheus* finale, so insistent that the death of Orpheus should be expressed with a conscious musical intensity to match that which he later granted unconsciously to Emmet, that he included a footnote on the competition score clarifying his expressive intentions "for the understanding of the performers". He explains that after the hero's death "the wind sighs mournfully and from time to time causes Orpheus' half-destroyed lyre to vibrate". A mountain shepherd tries to reproduce Orpheus' earlier hymn to love on his flute, "the wind dies down, little by little; the sounds it carried with it disappear; from the lyre one hears a few incoherent vibrations. Calm . . . silence . . . solitude".[173]

Perhaps 'a few incoherent vibrations' is all that we may expect of any death. Berlioz himself certainly expected no more, and would probably have responded to the above speculations with rational dismissal rather than romantic indulgence. As for reincarnation, the reader is reminded that this was only one of seven possibilities, while the author confesses that for all his advocacy he remains agnostic on the matter. But the oddities remain, awaiting alternative explanations, while there are four conjectures which an assiduous investigator of old diaries and letters might care to pursue: (1) Did anyone ever remark on a resemblance between Harriet Smithson and Sarah Curran? (2) Did Sarah ever wear pink boots? (3) Did Robert Emmet's father have old friends in the region of Grenoble? (4) Did Berlioz's heartfelt decision not to tamper with 'Élégie' coincide either with Moore's eulogy of Emmet in Dublin Castle in 1838, or with his proud recollection of the incident as he updated his journal on September 24th of that year?

*Last lines of 'Believe me, if all those endearing young charms' from *Irish Melodies*.

References

All authors quoted are listed in the bibliography and page numbers apply to editions detailed there. In cases where an author appears more than once in the bibliography, a shortened version of the relevant title is given here in brackets.

1 Berlioz (Memoirs) p.506
2 Berlioz (Memoirs) p.31
3 Barzun (Berlioz Vol.1) p.553
4 Berlioz (Memoirs) p.35
5 Berlioz (Memoirs) p.36
6 Berlioz (Memoirs) p.37
7 Barzun (Berlioz Vol.1) p.510
8 Berlioz (Memoirs) p.31
9 Berlioz (New Letters) p.3
10 Berlioz (Memoirs) p.31/32
11 Barzun (Berlioz Vol.2) p.101
12 Berlioz (Memoirs) p.293
13 Berlioz (New Letters) p.177
14 Barzun (Berlioz Vol.2) p.94
15 Berlioz (Memoirs) p.163
16 Barzun (Berlioz Vol.1) p.212
17 Berlioz (Evenings) p.357
18 Berlioz (Evenings) p.32
19 Berlioz (Memoirs) p.31
20 Berlioz (Selection) p.79
21 Berlioz (Memoirs) p.407
22 Berlioz (New Letters) p.7
23 Berlioz (Memoirs) p.33
24 Berlioz (Selection) p.57
25 Barzun (Berlioz Vol.2) p.213
26 Barzun (Berlioz Vol.2) p.253
27 Berlioz (Memoirs) p.461
28 Berlioz (New Letters) p.157
29 Wotton, p.94
30 Barzun (Berlioz Vol.2) p.84
31 Berlioz (Memoirs) p.189
32 Berlioz (Selection) p.105
33 Turner, p.167
34 Berlioz (Memoirs) p.228
35 Berlioz (Travers Vol.3) p.153
36 Mendl, p.111
37 Barzun (Berlioz Vol.2) p.238
38 Halstead, p.161
39 Berlioz (Evenings) p.316
40 Berlioz (Evenings) p.270
41 Berlioz (Selection) p.51
42 Barzun (Berlioz Vol.1) p.569
43 Berlioz (Evenings) p.316
44 Wagner, p.23
45 Berlioz (Memoirs) p.460
46 Barzun (Berlioz Vol.2) p.213
47 Barzun (Berlioz Vol.2) p.19
48 Berlioz (Memoirs) p.169
49 Berlioz (Memoirs) p.169
50 Berlioz (Evenings) p.271
51 Berlioz (Memoirs) p.89
52 Berlioz (Memoirs) p.168

53 Weiss, p.323

54 Berlioz (Memoirs) p.431

55 Berlioz (New Letters) p.121

56 Berlioz (Memoirs) p.64

57 Turner, p.185

58 Berlioz (Travers Vol.1) p.6

59 Barzun (Berlioz Vol.1) p.135

60 Barzun (Berlioz Vol.1) p.135

61 Berlioz (Memoirs) p.253

62 Barzun (Berlioz Vol.1) p.199

63 Berlioz (New Letters) p.7

64 Berlioz (Selection) p.66

65 Barzun (Berlioz Vol.1) p.241

66 Turner, p.167

67 Berlioz (Memoirs) p.470

68 Berlioz (Memoirs) p.363

69 Berlioz (Memoirs) p.229

70 Berlioz (Evenings) p.234

71 Berlioz (Evenings) p.125

72 Berlioz (Memoirs) p.59

73 Berlioz (Selection) p.82

74 Berlioz (Travers Vol.2) p.161

75 Berlioz (Memoirs) p.59

76 Turner, p.260

77 Ganz, p.183

78 Berlioz (Selection) p.104

79 Ganz, p.59

80 Berlioz (Evenings) p.330

81 Berlioz (Memoirs) p.440

82 Berlioz (Memoirs) p.363

83 Gal, p.212

84 Barzun (Berlioz Vol.2) p.238

85 Berlioz (Memoirs) p.96

86 Berlioz (Memoirs) p.96

87 Berlioz (Selection) p.193

88 Berlioz (Memoirs) p.343

89 Berlioz (Treatise) various
   sections

90 Macdonald, p.9

91 Berlioz (Evenings) p.233

92 Berlioz (Evenings) p.235

93 Barzun (Berlioz Vol.2) p.327

94 Berlioz (Travers Vol.3) p.131

95 Berlioz (Travers Vol.3) p.129

96 Berlioz (Memoirs) p.475

97 Berlioz (Memoirs) p.478

98 Berlioz (Memoirs) p.478

99 Barzun (Berlioz Vol.2) p.275

100 Mowat, p.162

101 Berlioz (Selection) p.57

102 Berlioz (Memoirs) p.203

103 Barzun (Berlioz Vol.2) p.261

104 Barzun (Berlioz Vol.1) p.198

105 Barzun (Berlioz Vol.1) p.419

106 Berlioz (Evenings) p.183

107 Ganz, p.26

108 Delacroix, p.110

109 Berlioz (Travers Vol.1) p.12

110 Berlioz (Travers Vol.2) p.15

111 Berlioz (Travers Vol.1) p.71

112 Berlioz (Travers Vol.1) p.78

113 Lockspeiser, pp.20-29

114 Ahouse (Berlioz) p.18

115 Berlioz (Selection) p.37

116 Berlioz (Evenings) p.307

117 Berlioz (Memoirs) p.106

118 Berlioz (New Letters) p.221

119 Turner, p.355

120 Berlioz (Travers Vol.3) p.51

121 Berlioz (Evenings) p.230

122 Berlioz (Travers Vol.1) p.163

123 Brown, pp.164/178

124 Berlioz (Memoirs) p.393

125 Ahouse (Course) p.21

126 Ahouse (Course) p.15

127 Berlioz (Memoirs) p.166

128 Berlioz (Evenings) p.260

129 Berlioz (Memoirs) p.124

130 Berlioz (Memoirs) p.465

131 Berlioz (Travers Vol.3) p.136

132 Berlioz (Travers Vol.3) p.74

133 Berlioz (Travers Vol.3) p.165

134 Berlioz (Travers Vol.3) p.125

135 Berlioz (Memoirs) p.517

136 Berlioz (Travers Vol.3) p.134
137 Berlioz (Travers Vol.3) p.135
138 Gal, p.211
139 Berlioz (Memoirs) p.170
140 Berlioz (Memoirs) p.455
141 Cairns (Romantic Imagination)
   p.135
142 Berlioz (Memoirs) p.465
143 Berlioz (Memoirs) p.434
144 Berlioz (Memoirs) p.515
145 Barzun (Berlioz Vol.2) p.159
146 Berlioz (Travers Vol.1) p.24
147 Berlioz (Memoirs) p.462
148 Berlioz (Memoirs) p.462
149 Barzun (Berlioz Vol.2) p.220
150 Berlioz (Selection) p.149
151 Cairns (Responses) p.92
152 Berlioz (Evenings) p.309
153 Berlioz (Memoirs) p.92
154 Hartnoll, p.134
155 Cairns (Introduction) p.15
156 Berlioz (Memoirs) p.521
157 Davis
158 Cairns (Romantic Imagination)
   p.xiii
159 Berlioz (Memoirs), p.497
160 Wotton p.12
161 Klein p.15
162 Halstead p.142
163 Emmet, Landreth, O'Broin,
            Postgate, Reynolds
164 Reynolds, p.125
165 Berlioz (Memoirs) p.132
166 Reynolds, p.125
167 Berlioz (Memoirs) p.519
168 Wilmot p.54
169 Emmet (Vol.2) p.xiii
170 Stevenson
171 Stevenson, p.96
172 Berlioz (Sixty-One) p.51
173 Bloom, p.195

Bibliography

1. BOOKS BY BERLIOZ

A Travers Chants (3 vols., trans: Evans, London 1915-18, reprinted as below)
>   Vol. 1 — *A Critical Study of Beethoven's Nine Symphonies* (London 1958)
>   Vol. 2 — *Gluck and his Operas* (London 1972)
>   Vol. 3 — *Mozart, Weber and Wagner — with various essays on musical subjects* (London 1969)

A Treatise on Modern Instrumentation and Orchestration, with the *Chef d'Orchestre* appended (trans: Clarke, ed: Bennett, London n.d.)

Correspondance Inédite (included in vol. 1 of *Life and Letters* — see below)

Evenings with the Orchestra (trans: Barzun, Chicago, 1973)

Hector Berlioz — a Selection from his Letters (trans: Searle, London 1966)

Lettres Intimes (included in vol.2 of *Life and Letters* — see below)

Life and Letters (2 vols., trans: Dunstan, 1882)

Memoirs of Hector Berlioz (trans: Cairns, London 1969)

New Letters of Berlioz, 1830-1868 (trans: Barzun, N.Y. 1954)

2. BOOKS ABOUT BERLIOZ

AYRTON, M. *Berlioz — a Singular Obsession* (London 1969)

BARZUN, J. *Berlioz and the Romantic Century* (2 vols, London 1951)

CAIRNS, D.(Ed.) *Berlioz and the Romantic Imagination* (Arts Council exhibition catalogue, London 1969)

DANISKAS, J. *Hector Berlioz* (trans: Doyle — Davidson, Stockholm n.d.)

DICKINSON, A.E.F. *Music of Berlioz* (London 1972)

ELLIOT, J.H. *Berlioz* (London 1967)

GANZ, A.W. *Berlioz in London* (London 1950)

MACDONALD, H. *Berlioz Orchestral Music* (London 1969)

NEWMAN, E. *Berlioz, Romantic and Classic* (ed: Heyworth, London 1972)

PRIMMER, B. *The Berlioz Style* (London 1973)

SEROFF, V.I. *Hector Berlioz* (N.Y. 1967)

TURNER, W.J. *Berlioz, the Man and his Work* (London 1939)

WOTTON, T.S. *Hector Berlioz* (London 1935)

3. CULTURAL & HISTORICAL BACKGROUND

BARZUN, J. *Classic, Romantic and Modern* (N.Y. 1962)

BOAS, G. *French Philosophies of the Romantic Period* (N.Y. 1925/ 1964)

BOWLE, J. *Politics and Opinion in the 19th Century* (London 1954)

BRIGGS, A. (Ed.) *The Nineteenth Century: the contradictions of progress* (London 1970)

CHARLTON, D.G. *Secular Religions in France, 1815-1870* (London 1963)

CHARVET, P.E. *A Literary History of France, Vol. 4: The Nineteenth Century 1789-1870* (London 1967)

COBBAN, A. *A History of Modern France, Vol.2: 1789-1871* (London 1965)

CROCE, B. *History of Europe in the Nineteenth Century* (trans: Furst, London 1965)

EINSTEIN, A. *Music in the Romantic Era* (London 1947)

FLEMING, W. *Arts and Ideas* (N.Y. 1968)

FURST, L.R. *Romanticism in Perspective* (London 1969)

HALSTEAD, J.B. (Ed.) *Romanticism* (N.Y. 1969)

HAUSER, A. *The Social History of Art* — Vols. 3 & 4 (London 1962)

HOBSBAWM, E.J. *The Age of Revolution 1789-1848* (London 1962)

KELLY, L. *The Young Romantics: Paris 1827-37* (London 1976)

LOCKE, A.W. *Music and the Romantic Movement in France* (London 1920)

MOSSE, G.L. *The Culture of Western Europe: the 19th and 20th centuries* (London 1963)

MOWAT, R.B. *The Romantic Age: Europe in the early 19th century* (London 1937)

PECKHAM, M. (Ed.) *Romanticism, the Culture of the Nineteenth Century* (N.Y. 1966)

SCHENK, H.G. *The Mind of the European Romantics* (London 1966)

SOLTAU, R.H. *French Political Thought in the 19th Century* (N.Y. 1959)

TALMON, J.L. *Romanticism and Revolt* (London 1967)

4. OTHER SOURCES CONSULTED OR QUOTED

AHOUSE, J. *Berlioz and Odoevsky* (Bulletin of the Berlioz Society, London, July 1975)

AHOUSE, J. *The 'Course a l'Abîme' : a Possible Source* (Bulletin of the Berlioz Society, London, April/July 1974)

BERLIOZ, H. *Vocal works* — English translations of various passages (used for performance, issued with recordings, etc.)

BERLIOZ, H. *Sixty-One Letters* ('Adam International Review' Nos. 331-333, N.Y. 1969)

BLOOM, P.A. *Orpheus' Lyre Resurrected: a tableau musical by Berlioz* ('The Musical Quarterly', N.Y. April 1975)

BOLSTER, R. *French Romanticism and the Ireland Myth* ('Hermathena' Vol. 98-99, Dublin 1964)

BROWN, R. *Unfinished Symphonies — voices from the beyond* (London 1971)

BYRON, G. *Poetic Works* (many editions)

CAIRNS, D. *Introduction* to a version of Berlioz's *Evenings in the Orchestra* not otherwise quoted (ed: Fortescue, London 1963)

CAIRNS, D. *Responses — musical essays and reviews* (London 1973)

CARLYLE, T. *Essays* (many editions)

CHATEAUBRIAND, F-R. *The Memoirs of Chateaubriand* (trans: Baldick, London 1961)

CONE, E.T. (Ed.) *Hector Berlioz — Fantastic Symphony*: score, background, analysis, views, comments (London 1971)

DAVIS, C. *Hector Berlioz, our Contemporary* (spoken contribution, colloquiem at French Institute, London, October, 1969)

DELACROIX, E. *Journal of Eugène Delacroix* (trans: Norton, ed: Wellington, London 1951)

ELLIOTT, J.R. *The Shakespeare Berlioz Saw* ('Music & Letters', London, July 1976)

EMMET, T.A. *Memoir of Thomas Addis and Robert Emmet* (2 vols., N.Y. 1915)

GAL, H. (Ed.) *The Musician's World — great composers in their letters* (London 1965)

HARTNOLL, P. (Ed.) *Shakespeare in Music* (London 1966)

JOHNSON, S. *Lives of the English Poets* (many editions)

KLEIN, J.W. *Berlioz's Personality* ('Music & Letters', London, January 1969)

LANDRETH, H. *The Pursuit of Robert Emmet* (Dublin 1949)

LOCKSPEISER, E. *Music and Painting* (London 1973)

MENDL, R.W.S. *The Divine Quest in Music* (London 1957)

MOORE, T. *Poetic Works* (many editions)

MOORE, T. *Memoirs, Journal and Correspondence* (various editions)

O'BROIN, L. *The Unfortunate Mr. Robert Emmet* (Dublin 1958)

POSTGATE, R.W. *Robert Emmet* (London 1931)

REYNOLDS, J.J. *Footprints of Emmet* (Dublin 1903)

SHAKESPEARE, W. *Plays* (many editions)

SHELLEY, P.B. *Poetry and Prose* (many editions)

SHRADE, L. *Beethoven in France — the growth of an idea* (Yale 1942)

STASOV, V. *Selected Essays on Music* (trans: Jonas, London 1968)

STEVENSON, I. *Twenty Cases Suggestive of Reincarnation* (N.Y. 1966)

WAGNER, R. *Stories and Essays* (ed: Osborne, London 1973)

WEISS, P. (Ed.) *Letters of Composers Through Six Centuries* (Philadelphia 1967)

WILMOT, C. *An Irish Peer on the Continent, 1801-1803* (Ed; Sadleir, London 1920)

WORDSWORTH, W. *Poetic Works* (many editions)

Index

Aeneid (Virgil) 17, 127
Alfieri, Vittorio (1749-1803) 88
Alizard, Louis (1814-50) 59, 115
Andrea Chénier (Giordano) 63
Anti-Semitism 36
Aquinas (St. Thomas) (1225-74) 88
Araudas, G. (See Ferrand)
Arnim, L. Achim (1781-1831) 64
Ascanio (Dumas) 84
Ascanio (Saint-Saens) 84
Atala (Chateaubriand) 29, 33, 87
Atheism 21, 24
Auden, W.H. (1907-73) 13
Austro-Prussian war (1866) 56, 114

Bacon, Francis (1561-1626) 78
Bacon, Roger (1214-94) 78
Balzac, Honoré (1799-1850) 15, 54, 86, 88
Barber of Seville (Rossini) 79
Barbier, Auguste (1805-82) 84, 88, 104
Barzun, Jacques (b.1907) 13, 75, 104
Beauvoir, Roger (1806-66) 88
Beccaria, Cesare (1738-94) 40, 88
Beethoven, Ludwig van (1770-1827) 10, 11, 15, 17, 34, 55, 63, 64, 68, 76, 79, 80, 85, 90, 102, 106, 109
Bellini, Vincenzo (1801-35) 15
Béranger, P-J. (1780-1857) 88
Berlioz, Louis Hector (1803-69)
 RELATIVES
  Maternal Grandfather (Nicholas Marmion, ? - 1837) 16
  Father (Louis-Joseph, 1776-1848) 15, 16, 19, 25, 38, 100, 109, 120
  Mother (Marie, 1784-1838) 16, 25, 40, 109
  Sister 1 (Nanci, 1806-50) 18, 37

  Sister 2 (Adèle, 1814-60) 37, 108
  First wife (see Harriet Smithson)
  Second wife (see Marie Recio)
  Son (Louis, 1834-67) 16, 38, 109
 CHARACTERISTICS
  Artistic interests 81, 82
  Authors featured in music 87, 88
  Childhood 16-19
  Conducting 68, 79
  Dress 39
  Education 16, 18, 19
  Ethics 24, 37, 19
  Humanitarian traits 23, 36, 37-39, 47, 56, 110, 112
  Humour 22, 35, 78, 79
  Idealism 20, 75, 78, 79, 85, 94, 96-98, 110
  Intellect 19, 77, 79
  Internationalism 54-57, 110
  Isolation (sense of) 20, 28, 91, 94, 95, 100, 108
  Languages 17, 104, 120
  Letters 68, 89, 125
  Literary interests 17, 19, 24, 86, 88, 101, 103
  Love-life 17-19, 60, 99-101
  Love of Nature 16, 19, 27, 29, 82
  Miscellaneous interests 77, 87, 89, 90
  Morality 38, 40, 109
  Musical criticism 48, 78, 89
  Musical enthusiasms 18, 76, 102, 106
  Musical expressiveness 34, 67, 68-74
  Musical opinions 75
  Musical style 69, 76
  Pacifism 38, 56, 110

Personality 107-109, 118
Philosophy 26, 78, 80
Politics 19, 42-47, 48-57, 110
Rationalist traits 21-26, 37, 53,
    78, 79, 89
Religion 18, 19, 21, 27-35, 92,
    103, 106, 110, 112, 126
Romantic traits 53, 75, 80, 81,
    85, 89, 95, 98, 112
Scepticism 19, 21-26, 90, 112
Social attitudes 36, 37-41, 95,
    112
Stoicism 25, 98
Suicidal streak 19, 99, 101˙
Writings 12, 79
LITERARY WORKS
A Travers Chants 89
Chef d'Orchestre 68
Evenings with the Orchestra 34,
    53, 84, 89
Grotesques de la Musique 89
Memoirs 12, 16, 19, 23, 25, 26,
    45, 46, 49, 58, 78, 83, 84,
    89, 93, 98, 99-102, 106, 109,
    117
*Treatise on Instrumentation and
    Orchestration* 35, 51, 68-74,
    89
MUSICAL WORKS
'Absence' (from *Nuits d'Eté*) 101
Apothéose 45, 53
Beatrice & Benedict 88, 108
Benvenuto Cellini 39, 84, 88
'Chant Guerrier' (from *Irlande*)
    116
Corsaire Overture 83
Damnation of Faust 28, 35, 39,
    55, 81, 88, 91, 101, 104
Death of Cleopatra 69, 101
Death of Ophelia 100
Death of Orpheus 72, 127, 128
'Elégie' (from *Irlande*) 58-61, 72,
    115-118, 120, 121, 128
Eight Scenes from Faust 28, 91
Fantastic Symphony 19, 27, 29,
    35, 58, 63, 69, 71, 87, 88,
    100, 125
Fifth of May 45
Francs-Juges 63
*Funeral and Triumphal Sym-
    phony* 45, 73, 116
Funeral March for Hamlet 100
Grande Messe des Morts
    (see *Requiem*)
Harold in Italy Symphony 27,
    70, 88, 95
Heroic Scene 46

Hymne à la France 45
Irlande 58, 59, 88, 120
Infant Christ 32, 88, 112
King Lear Overture 99
'King of Thule' (from *Damna-
    tion of Faust*) 101
Last Day of the World (projected
    only) 34
Lélio 58, 65, 70, 72, 97, 106,
    127
'L'Origine de la Harpe' (from
    Irlande) 120
Nuits d'Eté 80, 88, 101
Neuf Mélodies (see also *Irlande*)
    58, 116, 125
Presentation of the Colours
    (March for) 71
Railway Cantata 77
Rákóczy March 46
Religious Meditations 32, 65,
    100
Requiem 29, 30, 34, 49, 51, 70,
    72, 73, 88
Resurrexit 30
Reverie and Caprice 12
Roman Carnival Overture 39
Romeo and Juliet Symphony
    27, 30, 70, 72, 85, 88, 101
Sara la Baigneuse 40
Sardanapale 44
'Spectre de la Rose' (from *Nuits
    d'Eté*) 101
Star of Liberty (see *Temple
    Universel*)
'Sur les Lagunes' (from *Nuits
    d'Eté*) 101
Te Deum 30, 71, 73, 74, 88
Tempest Fantasia 70
Temple Universel 56
Toccata (last of three pieces for
    harmonium) 12
Tristia 101
Trojans 17, 37, 71, 88, 97, 101,
    104, 105, 108, 127
Waverley Overture 63
Berlioz and the Romantic Century
    (Barzun) 13
Bible, 23, 88
Bismarck, Otto (1815-98) 110
Blake, William (1754-1827) 108
Blanc, Louis (1811-82) 53
Boileau (-Despréux) N. (1636-1711)
    88
Bonald, Louis (1754-1840) 43
Bonaparte, Napoleon (1769-1821)
    (see Napoleon I)
Bossuet, J-B. (1627-1704) 88

Bougainville, L-A. (1729-1814) 88
Brentano, Clemens (1778-1842) 64
Brizeux, Auguste (1803-58) 88
Bunting, Edward (1773-1843) 64
Bürger, G.A. (1747-94) 91
Burke, Edmund (1729-97) 10, 54
Burns, Robert (1759-96) 64
Byron, Lord George (1788-1824)
 10, 17, 46, 65, 83, 88, 93-95

Cabanis, Georges (1757-1808) 24, 88
Cairns, David (b.1926) 107, 108
Calvin, John (1509-64) 23, 34
Camoëns, L.V. (1524-80) 85, 88
Capitalism 51
Carlyle, Thomas (1795-1881) 12
Catholicism 18, 21, 23, 30, 34, 126
Cavour, C.B. (1810-61) 110
Cellini, Benvenuto (1500-71) 84, 88
Cendrier, F-A (1803-92) 47
Censorship 24, 47
Cervantes (Saavedra), M. (1547-1616)
 85, 88
Charles VI (reigned France
 1380-1422) 55
Charles VI (Halévy) 55
Charles X (reigned France 1824-30)
 43, 44
Chartism, 53, 54
Chateaubriand, F-R. (1768-1848)
 10, 15, 29, 33, 41, 62, 77, 88
Chénier, André (1762-94) 62
Cherubini, M.L. (1760-1842) 79
Chevalier, Michel (1806-79) 55
Childe Harold's Pilgrimage (Byron) 95
Chopin, Frédéric (1810-49) 10
Christianity 18, 30, 33
Christian-socialism 41
Church of Humanity 104
Cimarosa, Domenico (1749-1801)
 75, 119
Clergy 22
Cobden, Richard (1804-65) 55
Coleridge, S.T. (1772-1834) 10, 30
Columbus, Christopher (1451-1506)
 85
Commercialism 46, 48, 94, 110
Commune (Paris, 1871) 57
Communist Manifesto (Marx &
 Engels) 52
Comte, Auguste (1798-1857) 15, 25
Comte Ory, Le (Rossini) 79
Concordat (Papal, 1801) 33
Condillac, Etienne (1715-80) 24
Condorcet, J. A-N (1743-94) 104
Confession of a Child of the Century
 (de Musset) 88

Confessions (Rousseau) 87
*Confessions of an English Opium
 Eater* (de Quincy) 87
Congress of Vienna (1814-15) 42
Cooper, J. Fenimore (1789-1851) 83,
 88
Corneille, Pierre (1606-84) 88
Corsair (Byron) 83
Cousin, Victor (1792-1867) 104
Cowley, Abraham (1618-67) 108
Cromwell (Hugo) 80
Curran, Sarah (1782-1808) 61, 65,
 115, 119, 123, 125, 126, 128

Dante (Alighieri) (1265-1321) 10
Darwin, Charles (1809-82) 15
Daumier, Honoré (1808-79) 15
David, Félicien (1810-76) 40
Davis, Colin (b.1927) 108, 112
Dean, Winton (b.1916) 107
Defence of Poetry (Shelley) 85
Deism 24, 103
D'Allemagne (Mme. de Stäel) 44
Delacroix, Eugène (1798-1863) 15,
 80, 103
De Maistre (see Maistre)
Democracy 48, 110
De Quincy, Thomas (1785-1859) 87,
 88
Der Freischütz (Weber) 32, 72, 87
Deschamps, A-F-M (1800-69) 45, 88
Deschamps, Emile (1791-1871) 31
Despotism 51
Disraeli, Benjamin (1804-81) 15
Doktor Faust (Heine) 96
Don Giovanni (Mozart) 72, 96
Duboeuf, Estelle (1797-1876) 17, 99,
 126
Du Boys, Albert (1804-89) 88
Duc, J-L (1802-79) 53
Dumas, Alexandre (elder) (1802-70)
 15, 84, 88, 103
Duveyrier, Charles (1803-66) 47

Eclecticism (philosophic) 104
Elijah (Mendelssohn) 35
Emerson, R.W. (1803-82) 15
Emmet, Robert (1778-1803) 61-67,
 90, 113-128
Emmet, Dr. R. (1729-1802) 113, 119,
 120, 124, 128
Emmet, T.A. (1764-1827) 114, 121,
 124
Enfantin, B-P (1796-1864) 25
Enlightenment (18th century) 37,
 80, 110
Equality 41

Eroica Symphony (Beethoven) 15
Escudier, Léon (1821-81) 118
Essay on the Inequality of Human Races (Gobineau) 36
Essay on the music of Ireland (Moore) 67
Estelle et Némorin (Florian) 17
Euphonia (imaginary country) 34, 51, 75, 89, 94, 99
Euripides (485-406 B.C.) 88

Faust legend 91, 96
Fauste (Goethe) 91
Ferrand, Humbert (1805-68) 34, 35, 49, 88
Fidelio (Beethoven) 96
Field, John (1782-1837) 65
Flaubert, Gustave (1821-80) 86, 88, 94
Florian, J-P (1755-94) 88
Flotow, Friedrich (1812-83) 64
Folk culture 63, 64
Fornier, Estelle (*née* Duboeuf) 99-101
Francis II Rákóczi, Prince of Transylvania (1676-1735) 47
Franco-Prussian war (1870) 57
French Revolution (see Revolution)
Freud, Sigmund (1856-1939) 109

Gall, F.J. (1758-1828) 24, 88
Garibaldi, Giuseppe (1807-82) 15
Garrick, David (1717-79) 30, 31
Gautier, Théophile (1811-72) 80, 88, 103
Genius of Erin (Emmet) 119
Giordano, Umberto (1867-1948) 63
Gladstone, W.E. (1809-98) 15
Glinka, Michael (1804-57) 15
Gluck, C.W. (1714-87) 10, 34, 76, 81, 94, 102
Gobineau, J-A (1816-82) 36
Goethe, J.W. (1749-1832) 10, 17, 28, 63, 87, 88, 91, 94
Gogol, N.V. (1809-52) 15
Gossec, F-J (1734-1829) 45
Gounet, Thomas (1801-69) 59
Great Exhibition (1851, London) 50, 69
Grimm, Jakob (1785-1863) 64
Grimm, Wilhelm (1786-1859) 64
Guérin, Léon (1807-?) 88

Halévy, J.F.F.E. (1779-1862) 55
Hamlet (Shakespeare) 58, 104
Haussonville, Louise (de Broglie) (?) 119
Haydn, Joseph (1732-1809) 10, 34, 64

Heaven 18, 25, 104
Hegel, G.W.F. (1770-1831) 104
Heine, Heinrich (1797-1856) 15, 23, 82, 88, 91, 94
Henry VIII (reigned England 1509-47) 22
Herder, J.G. (1744-1803) 10, 15, 64, 88
Hernani (Hugo) 44, 80, 87
Hiller, Ferdinand (1811-85) 35
Hitler, Adolf (1889-1945) 36
Hoffmann, E.T.A. (1776-1822) 79, 88
Horace (65-8 B.C.) 88, 109
Hugo, Victor (1802-85) 15, 17, 40, 44, 45, 47, 52, 53, 80, 87, 88, 103
Hume, David (1711-76) 78
Hunt, Leigh (1784-1859) 66

Idéologues 15, 24, 65
Industrial Revolution 10
Ingres, J-A-D (1780-1867) 81
Irish Melodies (Moore) 58, 59, 63, 67, 116
Irving, Washington (1783-1859) 115

Jacobinism 44, 47
Janin, Jules (1804-74) 77, 88
Jeune France party 44
Johnson, Samuel (1709-84) 108
Journal (Moore) 115
Judaism in Music (Wagner) 36
July Monarchy (1830-48) 45, 48
July Revolution (1830)
  (see Revolution)
Jung, C.G. (1875-1961) 122

Kant, Immanuel (1724-1804) 10, 15, 104
Kardec, Allan (1804-69) 90
Kemble, Charles (1775-1854) 31

La Bohème, (Puccini) 11
La Fontaine, Jean (1621-95) 88
Lalla Rookh (Moore) 64
Lamarck, J-B (1774-1829) 15
Lamartine, A-M-L de P. (1790-1869) 29, 47, 88
Lamennais, F-R (1782-1854) 41, 43, 47, 88
Last Rose of Summer (Moore) 64
Lebrun, P-D.E. (1729-1807) 88
Legouvé, Ernest (1807-1903) 107, 119
Lenore (Bürger) 91
Lenz, Wilhelm (1809-83) 35
Leonora Overture (Beethoven) 81
Leroux, Pierre (1797-1871) 104

Lesueur, J-F (1760-1837) 45, 86
Let Erin Remember (Moore) 116-118
Leuven, Adolph (1807-84) 88
Liberty Leading the People
  (Delacroix) 80
Lichnovsky, Felix (1814-48) 50
Lincoln, Abraham (1809-65) (U.S.
  President 1861-65) 15, 61
Liszt, Franz (1811-86) 10, 25, 35, 48
Livy (59 B.C. - 17 A.D.) 88
Locke, John (1632-1714) 24, 78
Longfellow, H.W. (1807-82) 15
Louis XVIII (reigned France 1814-24)
  43
Louis-Napoleon (1808-73)
  (see Napoleon III)
Louis-Philippe (1773-1850, reigned
  France 1830-48) 45, 48, 55
Loves of the Angels (Moore) 64
Lucan (39-65) 88
Luther, Martin (1483-1546) 23, 34,
  50

Macdonald, Hugh (b. 1940) 71
Macpherson, James (1736-96) 63
Maistre, Joseph (1753-1821) 43
Mahler, Gustav (1860-1911) 72
Malmoe Truce (1848) 50
Marseillaise (Rouget de Lisle) 45, 80,
  116
Martha (Flotow) 64
Martin, John (1798-1854) 82
Marx, Karl (1818-83) 52
Mezzini, Giuseppe (1805-72) 15, 46,
  110
Méhul, E-N (1763-1817) 45
Melologue Upon National Music
  (Moore) 65
Memoirs (Moore) 116
Mendelssohn, Moses (1729-86) 36
Mendelssohn (-Bartholdy), F.
  (1809-47) 10, 15, 22, 33, 34, 35,
  64, 79, 82
Merchant of Venice (Shakespeare) 105
Mesmer, F.A. (1734-1815) 104
Metternich, Prince K.W.N.L.
  (1773-1859) 47
Meyerbeer, Giacomo (1791-1864)
  70, 105
Michelangelo (Buonarotti) (1475-
  1564) 81
Michelet, Jules (1798-1874) 65
Mill, J.S. (1806-73) 15
Minstrel Boy (Moore) 64
Moke, Camille (1811-75) 19, 46, 99
Molière, J-B, P. (1622-73) 88
Monarchism 50, 51

Montesquieu, C. de S. (1689-1755)
  119
Moore, Thomas (1779-1852) 17, 25,
  32, 58-67, 88, 101, 114-116,
  120, 122, 125-128
Morgan, Sydney (1783-1859) 65
Mozart, W.A. (1756-91) 10, 34, 85,
  119
Much Ado About Nothing
  (Shakespeare) 108
Musical instruments 69-73
Musset, Alfred de (1810-57) 87, 88

Napoleon I (Bonaparte, reigned
  France 1804-14) 15, 24, 33, 42,
  45, 62, 114, 119, 121
Napoleon III (Louis-Napoleon,
  reigned France 1852-70) 43, 52
  55
Nationalism 42, 45, 54, 55, 64, 110
Nerval, Gérard (1808-55) 91, 103
New Christianity (Saint-Simon) 25
Novalis (F. von Hardenberg, 1772-
  1801) 10

O'Connell, Daniel (1775-1847) 54
Odoevsky, V.F. (1803-69) 82
Oh! Breathe not his name (Moore)
  115
On History (Carlyle) 12
Origin of the Harp (Moore) 120
Orphée (Gluck) 81, 127
Orpheus legend 127, 128
Ortigue, J-L (1802-66) 34, 88
Osborne, George (1806-93) 66
Ossian (third century?) 63, 65
Ovid (43 B.C. - 18 A.D.) 88

Pantheism 23, 28
Papacy 33, 41
Paradise and the Peri (Schumann)
  64
Pastoral Symphony (Beethoven) 81
Paul et Virginie (St. Pierre) 24
Pavlov, I.P. (1849-1936) 25
Percy, Thomas (1729-1811) 64
Philistinism 20, 40, 93, 96-98
Pius VII (reigned as Pope 1800-23)
  33
Plato (428-348 B.C.) 104
Pleyel, Camille (1788-1855) 99
Poe, E.A. (1809-49) 15
Poetry 19, 85, 101, 102
Positivism 25, 104, 111
Poussin, Nicholas (1593/4-1665) 81
Power, James (1766-1836) 64
Prinzhofer, August (1817-85) 39

Prix de Rome 19, 44, 69, 72, 101
Progress 77, 104
Prokofiev, Serge (1891-1953) 96
Protestantism 23, 126
Puccini, Giacomo (1858-1924) 11
Puritanism 23, 126
Pushkin, Alexander (1799-1837)
    15, 87

Racine, Jean (1639-99) 88
Recio, Marie (1814-62) 37, 100, 108
'Red Fox' (traditional Irish air) 116,
    117
Red Rover (Fenimore Cooper) 83
Reform Bill (1832) 46
Reincarnation 122, 124, 125, 128
Reliques of Ancient English Poetry
    (Percy) 64
René (Chateaubriand) 29, 33, 87
Republicanism 42, 48, 50
Return of the Emperor (Hugo) 45
Revolution (1789) 10, 48, 63, 110
Revolution (1830) 34, 44, 46, 53,
    80, 117
Revolution (1848) 41, 47, 52, 54
Robespierre, F-M-J (1758-94) 62
Roman Carnival 38, 39, 94
Romanticism 10, 11, 32, 63, 65, 80,
    91, 111
Romberg, Heinrich (1802-59) 51
Romeo and Juliet (Prokofiev) 96
Romeo and Juliet (Shakespeare) 30,
    85
Rossini, Gioacchino (1792-1868) 79
Rouget de Lisle, C-J (1760-1836) 45
Rousseau, J-J (1712-78) 10, 24, 87,
    89, 103

Sacred Songs (Moore) 25, 32
Saint-Beuve, C-A (1804-69) 15, 48
St. Paul (Mendelssohn) 35
Saint-Pierre (Bernardin), J-H
    (1737-1814) 24, 89
Saint-Saëns, Camille (1835-1921)
    84, 109
Saint-Simon, C-H (1760-1825) 19,
    25, 43, 48
Saint-Simonism 25, 43, 47, 56, 104
Salambô (Flaubert) 86
Sand, George (1804-76) 15, 47, 48,
    88, 91
Sax, Adolphe (1814-94) 49, 69, 84
Sayn-Wittgenstein, Carolyne
    (1819-87) 25, 35, 56, 105
Schelling, F.W.J. (1775-1854) 10
Schiller, J.C.F. (1759-1805) 17, 89
Schlegel, A.W. (1767-1845) 10

Schlegel, Friedrich (1772-1829) 10
Schleiermacher, F.E.D. (1768-1834)
    111
Schubert, Franz (1797-1828) 15
Schumann, Robert (1810-56) 10, 64,
    78
Scott, Walter (1771-1832) 10, 63,
    64, 88
Scribe, Eugène (1791-1861) 23
Second Empire (1852-70) 43, 52
Second Republic (1848-52) 53
Secular religions 103
Senancour, E.P. (1770-1846) 10
Shakespeare, William (1564-1616)
    10, 17, 31, 58, 63, 85, 88, 97,
    100-104, 106
She is Far from the Land (Moore) 115
Shelley, P.B. (1792-1822) 65, 85, 94,
    115
Sketch Book (Irving) 115
Smithson, Harriet (1800-54) 19, 49,
    58, 60, 63, 65, 99, 101, 103,
    123-125, 128
Socialism 41, 43, 53, 104
Socrates (470-399 B.C.) 103
Sophocles (496-406 B.C.) 97
Southey, Robert (1774-1843) 115
Spinoza, Benedict (1632-77) 104
Spirit of Christianity (Chateaubriand)
    33
Spiritualism 90, 104
Spontini, G.L.P. (1774-1851) 76, 102
Staël, Germaine de (1766-1817) 10,
    44, 119
Stendhal, (Beyle, H.) (1783-1842)
    65, 94
Stevenson, Ian (b.1918) 123
Stevenson, J.A. (1761-1833) 64
Strauss, Richard (1864-1949) 68
Sturm und Drang 10, 44
Swedenborg, Emmanuel (1688-1722)
    104
Symphony No. 5 (Beethoven) 86

Talleyrand (Périgord), C-M.
    (1754-1838) 114
Tasso, Torquato (1544-95) 85, 88
Taxation 48, 49
Tennyson, Alfred (1809-92) 15
Theophilanthropy 103
Theosophy 104
Thomson, George (1757-1851) 64
Toussaint l'Ouverture (1743-1803)
    62
Treaty of Amiens (1802) 115
Treaty of Commerce (1860) 55
Turner, J.M.W. (1775-1851) 94

Ultras (political Right) 41, 43
United Irish Movement 114, 117, 120
Universal Exhibition (1855, Paris) 74

Vaudin, J.F. (?) 56, 88
Verdi, Giuseppe (1813-1901) 10
Verne, Jules (1828-1905) 89
Vernet, E-J-H (1789-1863) 82
Viardot, Pauline (1821-1910) 81
Vieillard (de Boismartin), P.A.
    (1778-1862) 88
Vigny, Alfred (1797-1863) 15, 25,
    88, 103
Virgil, (70-19 B.C.) 17, 88, 104, 106
Voltaire, F.M.A. (1694-1778) 89, 97
Voyage Round the World (Bougain-
    ville) 16

Wagner, Richard (1813-1883) 10, 27,
    36, 70, 75

Wailly, Léon (1804-63) 84
Washington, George (1732-99, U.S.
    President 1789-97) 103
Waverley (Scott) 63
Weber, C.M.F.E. (1786-1826) 10, 32,
    72, 76, 79, 102
Werther (Goethe) 87
When he who adores thee (Moore)
    59, 60, 65, 117, 123
William Tell (Rossini) 79
Wilmot, Catherine (1773-1824) 118
Words of a Believer (Lamennais) 41
Wordsworth, William (1770-1850)
    10, 62
Working class 41, 44, 46, 50, 52

Youth's Magic Horn (Arnim &
    Brentano) 64